W9-CZT-174

OTHER TITLES IN THE CODENOTES SERIES

CodeNotes® for XML

CodeNotes® for .NET

CodeNotes® for Java: Intermediate and Advanced Language Features

CodeNotes® for VB.NET

CodeNotes® for Web-Based UI

CodeNotes® for J2EE

Edited by GREGORY BRILL

CodeNotes® for J2EE

EJB, JDBC, JSP, and Servlets

NEW YORK

Published in the United States by Random House, Inc., New York, and simultaneously in Canada by Random House of Canada Limited, Toronto.

Library of Congress cataloging-in-publication data is available.

ISBN 0-8129-9190-7

Website address: www.atrandom.com
Printed in the United States of America on acid-free paper
2 4 6 8 9 7 5 3

First Edition

Using CodeNotes

PHILOSOPHY

The CodeNotes philosophy is that the core concepts of any technology can be presented in less than two hundred pages. Building from many years of consulting and training experience, the CodeNotes series is designed to make you productive in a technology in as short a time as possible.

CODENOTES POINTERS

Throughout the book, you will encounter CodeNotes Pointers (e.g., `J2010101`). These pointers are links to additional content available online at the CodeNotes website. To use a CodeNotes Pointer, simply point a web browser to www.CodeNotes.com and enter the Pointer number. The website will direct you to an article or an example that provides additional information about the topic.

CODENOTES STYLE

The CodeNotes series follows certain style guidelines:

- Code objects and code keywords are highlighted using a special font. For example: `java.lang.Object`.
- Code blocks, screen output, and command lines are placed in individual blocks with a special font:

```
//This is an example code block
```

WHAT YOU NEED TO KNOW BEFORE CONTINUING

The J2EE specification encompasses applications ranging from database access to web applications to e-mailing systems. Because the topics are so varied, the CodeNotes format is compressed and certain background information has been omitted. However, a significant number of examples and background articles can be found on the CodeNotes website.

Basic Java

The authors assume that you know Java basics, such as `for` and `while` loops, file I/O, import statements, `try/catch/finally` structure, throwing exceptions, interfaces, inheritance, and other core Java concepts.

If you are familiar with any other object-oriented programming language, such as C++, then you should be able to follow the ideas presented in the code examples, although specific details may be unclear.

Basic SQL and Relational Database Systems

Database access plays a key role in J2EE. If you are unfamiliar with basic SQL statements (Select, Insert, Update, and Delete), stored procedures (return values, in, out, and inout parameters), or general relational database concepts (such as one-to-one, many-to-one, and many-to-many relationships), we suggest you become familiar with these topics before proceeding to the JDBC and EJB chapters. A quick review can be found on the CodeNotes website CN J2000001.

HTML and Web Technologies

The JSP and Servlet components of J2EE deal explicitly with web content. In order to make the most of these sections, you should be familiar with basic HTML concepts, including standard tags (<html>, <body>, <br/>, tables, etc.) and forms (text boxes, buttons, get and post methods). Having an understanding of one or more web application paradigms (PHP, CGI-BIN, ASP, ColdFusion, etc.) will be helpful but is not required.

XML Basics

While XML isn't a critical component of J2EE, a basic grounding in XML tags and Document Type Definitions will be helpful in certain sections. Both XML and DTDs are used heavily in the deployment of J2EE applications. A short refresher of XML basics can be found on the CodeNotes website CN J2080001. For a full introduction to XML, as well as related technologies such as XSLT and XPath, see *CodeNotes for XML.*

About the Authors

ROBERT MCGOVERN works as a consultant, architect, and trainer for Infusion Development Corporation. He has worked on everything from large mortgage and stock trading systems to biomechanics data collection and analysis systems. Rob currently lives in New Jersey with his fiancée.

STUART CHARLTON is the Senior Java Architect and Trainer for Infusion Development Corporation. He has consulted and trained for software vendors, Silicon Valley startups, and large financial institutions in the United States, Canada, and Japan. Stuart was born in Canada and currently lives in Hoboken, New Jersey.

GREGORY BRILL is president of Infusion Development Corporation, a firm specializing in architecting global-securities-trading and analytic systems for several of the world's largest investment banks in the United States and Tokyo. He has written articles for *C++ Users Journal* and is the author of *Applying COM+*. He lives in New York City.

More information about the authors and Infusion Development Corporation can be found at www.infusiondev.com/codenotes.

Acknowledgments

First, thanks to John Gomez, who saw the potential of the CodeNotes idea before anyone else and introduced me to Random House. Without John, there would be no CodeNotes. John, you are a true friend, a real visionary. I'd also like to thank Annie LaFarge, who fearlessly championed the series and whose creativity, enthusiasm, and publishing savvy have been instrumental in its creation. Thank you to Mary Bahr, our unflappable editor, who paved the way and crafted the marketing. Thank you to Ann Godoff, whose strength, decisiveness, and wisdom gave CodeNotes just the momentum it needed. And, of course, the production, sales, and business teams at Random House, with particular thanks to Howard Weill, Jean Cody, and Richard Elman.

On the Infusion Development side, thank you to Rob McGovern and Stuart Charlton, the writers of this CodeNote, for their excellent work. Their depth of knowledge about J2EE, their diligence in research, and their dedication to the project have gone a very long way to making this an exceptional book. Thank you for the CodeNotes reviewers, who gave us invaluable feedback and suggestions on our early drafts. And thank you to the entire cast and crew of Infusion Development Corporation, who have supported and encouraged this venture throughout. I know CodeNotes was extremely trying, tough to do, and involved an awesome amount of research, writing, and editing. But here it is . . . as we envisioned it.

—Gregory Brill

Contents

CodeNotes® for J2EE

Chapter 1

INTRODUCTION

ORIENTATION, HISTORY, BACKGROUND

What Is the Java 2 Enterprise Edition (J2EE)?

Depending upon whom you ask, Java 2 Enterprise Edition (J2EE) is one of many things. A systems architect might tell you that J2EE is a platform and design philosophy for large enterprise systems. Your local server administrator might tell you that J2EE is a combination of vendor products, WAR, JAR, and EAR files. A developer might tell you that J2EE is marketing spin wrapping up a suite of toolkits. In fact, J2EE comprises three major components.

1. A conceptual definition for enterprise systems architecture. This definition provides a rigorous design philosophy for building large, scalable, web-enabled systems.
2. A collection of API extensions that relate to enterprise systems. These APIs range from e-mail access to database connectivity, bridging concepts as different as distributed computing and web-based applications.
3. A new deployment specification for packaging Java components into a single enterprise solution. Basic Java uses a simple "Java Archive" standard for packaging a set of common class objects into a single deployable file. J2EE extends this concept to Web Archive (WAR) and Enterprise Archive (EAR) formats

for deploying larger enterprise systems. This deployment specification includes support for role-based security.

History

In 1999, Sun announced a fundamental redefinition of the Java platform. Java had originally been designed as an all-encompassing "Write Once, Run Anywhere™" system; but Java applications rapidly exploded across a tremendous range of platforms, from smart cards to air conditioners (e.g., www.myappliance.com) to distributed, mission-critical enterprise systems. Obviously, the requirements for an offline payment system on a smart card are vastly different from those of an enterprisewide, web-enabled stock trading platform.

Sun initially supported the different platforms by providing a core SDK and an assortment of extension APIs. This approach rapidly became unwieldy, and Sun redefined the Java platform into three distinct versions: Java 2 Micro Edition (for embedded applications such as smart cards), Java 2 Standard Edition (for normal Java applications), and Java 2 Enterprise Edition (for large-scale, distributed, web-enabled applications).

The J2EE APIs

When the initial J2EE specification was announced, many of the enterprise APIs already existed as independent packages. Thus it is often difficult to tell whether an API is part of Java 2 Enterprise Edition or Java 2 Standard Edition, or is a stand-alone package, or is included in more than one edition. As the various Java editions mature and the literature catches up with the changes in the Java platform, these distinctions should become clearer.

The most important J2EE 1.2.1 components are:

- JDBC 2.0—JDBC is the primary mechanism for using Java to communicate with SQL-compliant databases. J2EE requires the JDBC 2.0 Optional Package, an extension to the core JDBC API included with the Java 2 Standard Edition. Chapter 3 explains the core concepts of JDBC and working with relational databases.
- Java Servlets 2.2—Servlets are server-side web programs that are primarily gateways between web interfaces and middle-tier components. Servlet technology is an essential component to building secure, scalable web-enabled systems. Chapter 5 covers fundamental Servlet concepts and provides the framework for JavaServer Pages.

- JavaServer Pages (JSP) 1.1—JavaServer Pages (Chapter 6) extend the power of Servlets by providing a simple mechanism for decoupling web content generation from application and business logic.
- Java Naming and Directory Interface (JNDI) 1.2—JNDI provides a transparent Java interface to various naming and directory services, including LDAP, NDS, DNS, and NIS(YP). JNDI is briefly covered (along with RMI and JavaMail, below) in Chapter 4, and extensively covered on the CodeNotes website.
- Remote Method Invocation (RMI)—J2EE supports distributed computing by providing interfaces for both CORBA and a proprietary Remote Method Invocation system. RMI can crosscommunicate with CORBA using the Internet Inter-ORB Operating Protocol (IIOP).
- JavaMail 1.1—The JavaMail API provides an interface for sending and receiving e-mail through standard systems such as SMTP and POP3. This CodeNote describes sending e-mail, and several examples for reading e-mail are available on the website CN J2010004.
- Enterprise JavaBeans (EJB) 1.1—A JavaBean is a small Java class that follows design rules for exposing member variables. Enterprise JavaBeans (Chapter 6) extend the JavaBean concept into the world of distributed computing. EJBs are used for encapsulating business logic in small, reusable packages that are easily configured into complex applications.
- Java Transaction API (JTA) 1.0—This component provides support for distributed transaction systems. The JTA provides a user-level interface for creating and managing transactions. The use of JTA is beyond the scope of this CodeNote, but several examples are available on the WebSite CN J2010001.
- Java Messaging Service (JMS) 1.0—Many enterprise systems rely on secure, reliable messaging systems for publish-subscribe and broadcast services. JMS provides an interface to these technologies. J2EE 1.2.1 requires that the API definitions be included with any J2EE-compliant server product, but does not require an actual implementation. Although JMS is not covered in this book, several articles on JMS can be found on the website CN J2010002.

Several additional components, such as the Java Authentication and Authorization Service (JAAS), are in draft form and will be included in the next J2EE release, version 1.3, which was in its final draft phase at the time of writing. Chapter 9 (Darkside) includes a brief discussion of several of these technologies.

Deployment Specification

A common belief is that J2EE is nothing more than a wrapper for a set of toolkits. However, J2EE does contain some new tools that are inherently part of the specification. These tools provide packaging for systems components. By extending the traditional Java Archive, or JAR file, into Web Archive (WAR) and Enterprise Archive (EAR) files, the J2EE deployment specification provides much greater flexibility for distributed enterprise systems.

In addition to packaging, the deployment specification also includes definitions for role-based security. Role-based security can define access to individual methods on EJBs and access to individual web pages in a WAR. These security settings can also be accessed programmatically inside EJBs, Servlets, and JSPs for finer-grained control.

Finally, the deployment specification includes support for environment variables maintained by the J2EE container. These variables can range from database access to e-mail connectivity to default parameters. Environment settings are accessible through a naming service and JNDI. The deployment specification is detailed in Chapter 8 (Packaging and Deployment).

ABOUT THE VENDOR

Sun Microsystems

Sun (www.sun.com) originally developed Java as a language for television "set top boxes," which were an instrumental component of the anticipated interactive TV explosion. Instead, the Internet and World Wide Web exploded and Java was quickly drawn into the realm of platform independent computing.

Sun's philosophy for Java consists of two key statements: "The Network is the Computer"™ and "Write Once, Run Anywhere"™. These two concepts are built into every aspect of Java and J2EE.

Vendors

JDBC, JSP, Servlets, and EJB all require components that are built by third-party vendors. These components must conform to the basic J2EE specification but can have dramatically different support for the extended features of J2EE. The following lists of vendors include many of the market leaders but are by no means exhaustive.

JDBC Drivers

Most database vendors provide a JDBC driver for their database. For example, if you are using an Oracle database, you should strongly consider using the Oracle JDBC driver. However, several companies provide cross-database-compliant drivers that are very feature-rich.

- Merant (www.merant.com) is a major player in JDBC driver development and has offerings for all of the major databases.
- Inet Software (www.inetsoftware.de) provides crossplatform JDBC drivers, including an SQL Server driver.

If you are in doubt when selecting a JDBC driver vendor, the best starting point is always Sun's JDBC driver database (industry.java.sun.com/products/jdbc/drivers).

Service Provider Interfaces

The Java Naming and Directory Interface uses Service Provider Interfaces to communicate with proprietary naming and directory services. Sun maintains a database of SPIs and vendors at: java.sun.com/products/jndi/serviceproviders.html.

Application Servers

The J2EE application server market is rapidly expanding and highly competitive. The market leaders are described below, and additional vendors can be found on the website CN J2010003.

- BEA Weblogic (www.bea.com) is the current market leader for Java application servers.
- IBM WebSphere (www4.ibm.com/software/webservers/appserv/) is another very popular Java application server.
- iPlanet Application Server (http://www.iplanet.com/products/iplanet_application/) is the J2EE offering from the Sun-Netscape alliance.
- Borland AppServer (www.borland.com/appserver/) has some of the best support for EJBs and is fully J2EE compliant.

Java Development Environments

While you do not need a development environment for Java or J2EE, most environments offer significant advantages over text editors, including automatic code generation for JavaBeans and enhanced support for EJBs, JSPs, and other J2EE components. These environments are among the most popular:

- Borland JBuilder 4 Enterprise (www.borland.com/jbuilder/)
- Sun's Forte for Java (www.sun.com/forte/)
- IBM's VisualAge for Java (www-4.ibm.com/software/ad/vajava/)
- WebGain VisualCafe (www.webgain.com/products/visual_ cafe/)

You can always develop Java code in a simple text editor such as Windows Notepad or Unix vi. However, many text editors have advanced features such as keyword coloring and parenthesis tracking:

- Emacs with the jde (jde.sunsite.dk/)
- SlickEdit (www.slickedit.com)
- Jext (www.jext.org/)
- Jpadpro (www.modelworks.com/)

NOMENCLATURE AND TERMINOLOGY

The J2EE architecture is based on four key concepts: components, archives, containers, and connectors. These concepts are used throughout J2EE. Figure 1.1 shows how these concepts relate graphically.

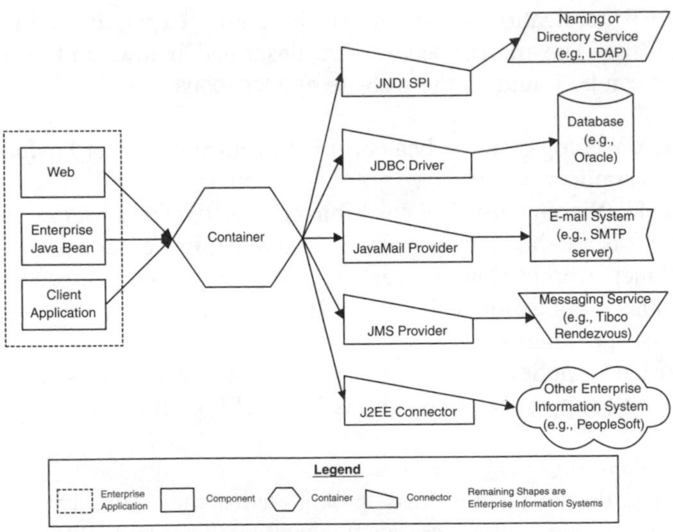

Figure 1.1 J2EE architecture

Components

A component is an individual Java object (class or JSP) or an archive of related Java objects. Components are the fundamental building blocks for J2EE and come in three flavors:

1. Web components such as JSPs, Servlets, or Web Archives.
2. EJB components, which are Java Archives containing EJB code and the deployment descriptor.
3. Client applications, which are stand-alone Java executables.

Archives

An archive is a package of Java code that contains one or more specific descriptors and a manifest. Deployment descriptors are the heart of the J2EE packaging specification. Descriptors provide configuration information, environment settings, role-based security, and vendor-specific information. The manifest is a packing slip that is automatically generated by the archive process.

J2EE defines three types of archives:

1. Java Archives (JAR)—A JAR file encapsulates one or more Java classes, a manifest, and a descriptor. JAR files are the lowest level of archive. JAR files are used in J2EE for packaging EJBs and client-side Java Applications.
2. Web Archives (WAR)—WAR files are similar to JAR files, except that they are specifically for web applications made from Servlets, JSPs, and supporting classes.
3. Enterprise Archives (EAR)—An EAR file contains all of the components that make up a particular J2EE application.

Containers

The container is an independent application that creates an environment for components. The container provides several key functions:

1. Life cycle management for components. The container instantiates new instances of a component and cleans up when the component dies.
2. Environment configuration. The container provides configuration information and the framework for the components.
3. Resources. The container also provides access to enterprise information systems such as databases, naming and directory services, and e-mail systems. This access is managed through connectors.

Connectors

The connector is where the abstract really meets the concrete. A connector is a translator between an enterprise information system and the J2EE interfaces. One type of connector, a JDBC driver, provides access to databases. Another type of connector, a JNDI Service Provider Interface, provides access to naming and directory services. The next version of J2EE is expected to standardize this area with the J2EE connector architecture.

Chapter 2

—

INSTALLATION

This chapter illustrates the process of installing J2EE and configuring Sun's reference implementation. Throughout the book, the J2EE reference implementation will be used as an example environment. If you already have a J2EE environment available, you can skip this chapter.

These instructions are written for Windows platforms. The instructions for most Unix systems follow the same pattern, although the download file and extraction programs are different.

HARDWARE

Sun's recommended system requirements for Java are on the low end for working with J2EE and any of the common development environments. We recommend the following:

- PC platforms: At least a Pentium II, 133 Mhz, 128 Mb RAM (256 preferred), running Windows 95/98/NT/2000/Me (NT/2000/Me preferred) or Linux
- Unix: Sun Ultrasparc (or equivalent Unix platform) with 256 Mb RAM
- Macintosh: G3 with 256 Mb RAM, running OS X or Linux PPC. Configuring the reference implementation for a Macintosh involves several unique challenges; some pointers can be found on the CodeNotes website CN J2020001.

NEAT TRICKS

If you are unfamiliar with working in a DOS environment inside of Windows, here are some useful tricks:

- To start a new command window, choose Run from the start menu and type "command" (if you are using Win95/98), or "cmd" (if you are using WinNT/2000).
- When you execute commands inside a Windows 95 or 98 shell, you may see error messages like "Out of environment space." These messages can be safely ignored. Windows will automatically allocate more space to the process. However, if you want to prevent these error messages, simply open a Windows shell, right-click on the title bar, and select properties from the drop-down menu. Select the memory tab. In the Conventional Memory area, increase the initial environment setting to 4096. Click the Apply button and then the OK button. Close the Windows shell. Any new Windows shell will start with more memory.
- When you need to start a process in the background, use the syntax "start *ProgramName [-options]*". This will launch the process in a new command window. If you don't preface the command with "start," you must create a new command window (and change to the proper directory) for each process. (For Unix developers, this is roughly equivalent to the syntax "*ProgramName [-options]* &".)

THE PLAN

The following sections of this chapter describe the installation and configuration of J2EE and the components of the reference implementation.

- Required installation—All J2EE applications require the J2SE Java Developers Kit, the J2EE Java Developers Kit, and configuration of several environment variables.
- Cloudscape—Cloudscape is the database component of the Java Reference Implementation. Several of the exercises in Chapter 3 (JDBC) are illustrated with Cloudscape.
- Web components—Both Servlets (Chapter 5) and JavaServer Pages (Chapter 6) require a container and an application. These chapters are illustrated with Tomcat (the container) and a basic Java web application called CodeNotes.

- Enterprise JavaBeans—EJBs require a significant amount of deployment, but no special steps are required for installation of the reference implementation.

You do not need to follow all of these instructions in order to get started with J2EE. Once you have completed the Required Installation section, feel free to jump ahead to Chapter 3 (JDBC) and return to this section when or if you need to set up the additional components.

REQUIRED INSTALLATION

Installing the J2SE Java Developers Kit (version 1.3.1)

All J2EE installations require that Java 2 Standard Edition (J2SE) be installed first. J2EE exists on top of J2SE and does not contain the core Java classes or the Java Virtual Machine (JVM). If you already have JDK 1.3 installed on your machine, you can skip this section.

1. Download the J2SE Java Developer Kit from Sun (java.sun.com/j2se/1.3/). The download file is about 30 Mb and should be called j2sdk-1_3_1-win.exe.
2. Download the JDK 1.3 documentation (java.sun.com/j2se/1.3/docs.html), which is about 20 Mb and called j2sdk-1_3_1-doc.zip.
3. Launch the j2sdk-1_3_1-win.exe file. This should start an InstallShield session.
4. After the welcome and license screens, you should have an option to choose an installation directory. You can place the JDK on any drive and in any directory. You should make a note of the directory name, as it will be important later. The default path is C:\jdk1.3, and the following instructions will assume you used this directory.
5. The fourth screen allows you to choose which components to install. Only the first two entries ("Program Files" and "Native Interface Header Files") are truly required. The "Old Native Interface Header Files" are provided as support for older versions of Java. The Demos are useful, but not required, and the Java Sources are provided in the spirit of "open source."
6. Continue with the installation, which should be fairly quick.
7. To install the documentation, use your favorite zip tool (e.g., WinZip) to unpack the j2sdk-1_3_1-doc.zip file. The documentation generally is placed in a \docs directory inside the JDK in-

stall directory (e.g., C:\jdk1.3\docs), although this is not a requirement. This file contains the complete JavaDocs for J2SE as well as release notes, documentation for the Java tools (rmic, javadoc, javac, etc.), and links to online documentation from Sun.

Installing the J2EE Software Development Kit (version 1.2.1)

The J2EE SDK installation is very similar to the J2SE installation. However, the J2EE SDK does not contain a Java Virtual Machine or any of the core Java functionality. If you have not already installed the J2SE JDK (v1.3), refer to the previous instructions before continuing.

1. Download the J2EE installation from java.sun.com/j2ee/j2sdkee/. The J2EE file for Windows is j2sdkee-1_2_1-win.exe (about 10 Mb).
2. Download the documentation file from the same web page. This file is called j2sdkee-1_2_1-doc-win.exe.
3. Start the installation by running j2sdkee-1_2_1-win.exe. This should start an InstallShield program.
4. After the welcome and license screens, you should have an option to choose an installation directory. You can place the J2EE SDK on any drive and in any directory. You should make a note of the directory name, as it will be important later. The default path is C:\j2sdkee1.2.1, and the following instructions will assume you used this directory.
5. Continue the installation. You don't have any choices as to program components, so the fourth screen is irrelevant. The remaining installation should be very quick.
6. To install the documentation, launch the j2sdkee-1_2_1-doc-win.exe file. This will start an InstallShield session that will automatically install the documentation in the \docs subdirectory of your J2EE installation directory (e.g., C:\j2sdkee1.2.1\docs.

Configuring the Environment

Certain J2EE applications require environment variables that are described below. The various versions of Windows have different methods for configuring environment variables:

- Windows 95/98—Edit the C:\autoexec.bat file. Open this file with Notepad or Wordpad. To set an environment variable, add an entry in the form:

```
SET VARIABLE=value1;value2;value3
```

These entries are very sensitive to extra spaces. When you have finished with your changes, save the file and restart Windows.

- Windows NT4—Right-click on the "My Computer" icon, select Properties, and then select the Environment tab.
- Windows 2000—Right-click on the "My Computer" icon, select Properties, select Advanced, then click the Environment Variables button.
- For both WinNT4 and Win2000, you have a graphical interface for adding and modifying environment variables. You also do not need to reboot after you make changes. On these platforms, add or edit the variables in the "User variables for *yourname*" section.

Regardless of your system version, you will need to add or update several variables. If the environment variable already exists on your system, check to see if the Java entry is already present. If the entry is not present, simply add a semicolon to the end of the existing entry and then add the new entry. If the variable doesn't exist, create it. Variable names should be fully capitalized.

- CLASSPATH—The JVM uses CLASSPATH to determine where the various Java files are located. Add the j2ee.jar file (e.g.,C:\j2sdkee1.2.1\lib\j2ee.jar) and the local directory ".". For Windows 95/98, the entry will look like:

```
SET CLASSPATH=.;C:\j2sdkee1.2.1\lib\j2ee.jar
```

- PATH—Many of the Java tools are stored in the bin directory of your JDK installation (e.g., C:\jdk1.3\bin). By adding this directory to your path file, you will have a much easier time accessing the Java compiler (javac), Java runtime (java), and other Java tools (javadoc, rmic, etc.).

```
SET PATH=C:\jdk1.3\bin
```

- J2EE_HOME—Various components of the reference implementation require a startup directory and base path for access to the J2EE components. This directory (e.g., C:\j2sdkee1.2.1) is called the J2EE_Home.

```
SET J2EE_HOME=C:\j2sdkee1.2.1
```

- JAVA_HOME—The JAVA_HOME variable should be set to the base installation directory for your Java Developers Kit (e.g., C:\jdk1.3)

```
SET JAVA_HOME=C:\jdk1.3
```

If you are working with Windows 95 or 98, don't forget to save the autoexec.bat file and restart your computer.

CLOUDSCAPE

Cloudscape is a simple SQL-92 relational database that is part of the Reference Implementation. Cloudscape is automatically installed as part of the J2EE Software Development Kit. To start Cloudscape, use the command:

```
start cloudscape –start
```

To stop Cloudscape, use the command

```
cloudscape –stop
```

WEB COMPONENTS

Both Chapter 5 (Servlets) and Chapter 6 (JavaServer Pages) are illustrated with examples that use the Tomcat container and a J2EE application called CodeNotes. This section covers the installation and configuration of Tomcat as well as the building of a basic web application.

JSP and Servlet Container

Tomcat

For demonstration purposes, this CodeNote will use the Tomcat Servlet and JSP engine, collaboratively developed by Sun and the Apache Foundation. Tomcat is available as a stand-alone package, although a modified version is included with the J2EE SDK. If you are already familiar with Tomcat or have access to a different JSP/Servlet container, feel free to skip ahead to the section "Creating a Web Application."

Installing the Software

Tomcat is very easy to install. For the sake of brevity, these instructions will demonstrate the installation of Tomcat on Windows (all versions). However, installations on other systems follow the same general steps, and specific instructions for Unix, Linux, and Solaris are available with the Tomcat download.

1. Go to `jakarta.apache.org/tomcat/index.html` and find the binary code for the most recent Release Build. The code examples were developed against Tomcat 3.2.1, although Tomcat 4.x is in development. For Windows systems, you should download the file jakarta-tomcat-3.2.1.zip (3 Mb). If you are installing on Linux, Unix, or Solaris, you will want to download the appropriate archive type (tar, gz, rpm, etc.).
2. Using you favorite zip tool, extract the contents of the file to your hard drive. You may put this directory anywhere you like (e.g., C:\Jakarta). You must use a command window to stop and start the server, however, so keep the path relatively short to save yourself some typing.
3. If you set JAVA_HOME in the Required Installation instructions, you can skip this step. In order for Tomcat to run, you must identify your Java directory in the tomcat.bat file, which can be found in the bin subdirectory under your install directory (e.g., C:\Jakarta\bin). Edit this file and find the "Save Environment Variables That May Change" section immediately after the first comments. Add a line like the following to identify your Java home directory:

```
SET JAVA_HOME=C:\jdk1.3
```

   This line is both case-sensitive and highly sensitive to spaces and syntax.

4. Save the tomcat.bat file. Tomcat is now installed.

Running Tomcat

Tomcat is a self-contained web server with support for Servlets and JSP. The default installation also includes some samples of JSPs and Servlet pages. Experimenting with these pages is a great way to test your installation.

1. Open a command window or browser and find the bin directory under your Tomcat installation directory (e.g., C:\Jakarta\bin).
2. Launch the startup.bat file (or startup.sh on Unix/Linux). This should open up a new command window. The startup.bat file sets a few key environment variables and then calls tomcat.bat.
3. DO NOT close the Tomcat command window! If you close the window, you will kill your Tomcat process. While this isn't generally a problem, it is much better to use the shutdown.bat script to stop Tomcat gracefully.
4. Once Tomcat has launched, open web browser and go to http://localhost:8080/. If your computer is part of a network, you can replace "localhost" with your computer name (e.g., "Dandelion" or "www.codenotes.com").

   Tomcat is set to run on port 8080 by default. Since HTTP generally runs through port 80, you must explicitly set the alternate port number in your URL (hence the ":8080" at the end of the example URL).
5. You should see a welcome page with some links to example pages, resources, and interest lists. Try out some of the example JSP and Servlet pages.

Creating a Web Application

Once you have your Tomcat server installed and running, you should create and register an application that you can use for web development. We are actually building a WAR (Web Archive) structure that is fully described in Chapter 8 (Packaging and Deployment). These instructions will get you started with a minimal application that you can use for both JSPs and Servlets.

1. Create a directory called webdev. This directory can be anywhere on your system (e.g., C:\webdev). This is the root-level directory for your application. You can place all of your JSP and HTML pages in this directory or use subdirectories to organize them. The following examples will use C:\webdev as the root directory. You can name this directory whatever you want, just remember to replace C:\webdev with your directory name in the following instructions.
2. From this point on, all file and folder names are mandatory and case-sensitive. In other words, the only choice you get to make is the name of the parent directory. All other names should be entered as specified, including punctuation and capitalization.
3. Create a directory called WEB-INF inside the webdev directory

(e.g., C:\webdev\WEB-INF). This directory will be used for storing configuration information.

4. Inside the WEB-INF directory, create a directory called classes (C:\webdev\WEB-INF\classes) and another called lib (C:\webdev\WEB-INF\lib). You will use these directories to store the Java code that will support your web pages. The classes directory is for Servlets, JavaBeans, and other compiled Java code, while the lib directory is for JAR packages.
5. Inside the WEB-INF directory, use the tool of your choice to create an XML file called web.xml. This configuration file is used to identify the application. The contents of the file should look like this:

```
<?xml version="1.0" encoding="ISO-8859-1"?>
<!DOCTYPE web-app
PUBLIC "-//Sun Microsystems, Inc.//DTD Web Application 2.2//EN"
"http://java.sun.com/j2ee/dtds/web-app_2.2.dtd">
<web-app>
</web-app>
```

Listing 2.1 Web.xml file

6. Save and close the web.xml file.

Configuring the Server

Once you have built your application directory and configuration file, you must configure the server to recognize the new application. This process is similar to registering a new website with any other web server. The exact syntax and steps for configuring the server depend on the vendor; however, most JSP/Servlet containers support a similar configuration mechanism.

1. If Tomcat is currently running, use the shutdown.bat file to stop it.
2. Find the server.xml file. It should be in the Tomcat home directory, under the conf subdirectory (e.g., C:\jakarta\conf\server .xml).
3. Edit the server.xml file and find the Context tag for the sample applications. It should be toward the bottom of the file in the "Special Webapps" section, and should look like this:

```
<Context path="/examples"
  docBase="webapps/examples"
```

```
  crossContext="false"
  debug="0"
  reloadable="true" >
</Context>
```

Listing 2.2 The Context node

4. Make sure that you select the stand-alone context rather than the one enclosed inside the virtual host example.
5. Create a new context node for your application by copying the context node from the examples application. Paste it into the server.xml file just below the examples application.
6. Change the path property. The path property is the base URL path for your application. You may choose any path you like, and it does not need to match the root folder for your application. Even though our example application is called webdev, we can set the path to "CodeNotes":

```
path="/CodeNotes"
```

When you create new JSPs or Servlets and place them in the webdev directory for your application, you can access them by pointing a web browser at:

```
http://localhost:8080/CodeNotes
```

If your computer is connected to a network and a domain name server, you can use your actual computer name (e.g., Dandelion) instead of localhost. Be aware that this URL is case-sensitive.

7. Change the docBase property. The docBase property tells Tomcat where your source files are located. Change the property to the directory where you have installed your application. For example, if you followed the Windows NT instructions above, the docBase directory would be

```
docBase="C:\webdev"
```

8. You should also add a few parameters that tell Tomcat about your application. These parameters are fully explained in the deployment section. Add these attributes to the `Context` node:

```
defaultSessionTimeOut="30"
isWARExpanded="true"
```

```
isWARValidated="false"
isInvokerEnabled="true"
isWorkDirPersistent="false"
```

Listing 2.3 Context node attributes

9. The `Context` node for your application should now look like this, with the exception of your specific path and docBase attributes:

```
<Context path="/CodeNotes"
  docBase="C:\webdev"
  defaultSessionTimeOut="30"
  isWARExpanded="true"
  isWARValidated="false"
  isInvokerEnabled="true"
  isWorkDirPersistent="false"
  debug="0"
  reloadable="true" >
</Context>
```

Listing 2.4 The CodeNotes application descriptor

10. Save and close the file.
11. Open a new command window and change to the bin directory in your Tomcat installation directory (e.g., C:\Jakarta\bin).
12. Start Tomcat using the startup.bat file. A new command window should open.
13. As Tomcat starts up, you should see a new line in the command window indicating that the ContextManager has added your context. For example:

```
2001-05-11 12:06:00 - ContextManager: Adding context Ctx(/CodeNotes)
```

    If you don't see this message, then your installation is not properly configured. Double-check your server.xml file and make sure that the `Context` node is correct. Pay particular attention to the docBase setting. Also, make sure that your `Context` node is not in the "Virtual Server Example" section or embedded in another set of tags.
14. At this point, any JSPs or Servlets you put into your application directory (e.g., C:\webdev) will be accessible via a web browser. Copy the snoop.jsp file from the Tomcat samples

directory (e.g., C:\jakarta\webapps\examples\jsp\snp) to your application directory (e.g., C\webdev).

15. Open a web browser and go to http://localhost:8080/CodeNotes/snoop.jsp. Both the application name (CodeNotes) and the JSP file name (snoop.jsp) are case-sensitive. The snoop.jsp page should display information about your browser.

ENTERPRISE JAVABEANS

The Enterprise JavaBeans reference implementation does not require any additional configuration or setup. The process of deploying an EJB, however, involves a considerable amount of configuration. EJB deployment is covered both in Chapter 7 (Enterprise JavaBeans) and Chapter 8 (Packaging and Deployment).

Chapter 3

JDBC

Eventually, every major enterprise software solution has to connect to a database. Whether the database is a central component, part of a legacy system, or record storage for a transactional messaging service, some amount of data will eventually be pushed to or pulled from a database.

Of course, connecting to and communicating with databases is not as simple a task as it should be. Database vendors use slightly different versions of the Structured Query Language (SQL) and the underlying databases may have wildly different features.

History

Every significant programming language has made one or more attempts to provide uniform access to relational database systems. On the Microsoft side alone, these attempts include ODBC, ADODB, DAO, and OLEDB. The major difficultly lies in providing a conventional programming language that can interact transparently with a variety of databases.

Traditional (pre-ODBC) solutions relied on language extensions where static SQL was embedded inside a language such as COBOL or C. Results were retrieved in static data structures. This kind of binding was very specific for each database vendor's particular SQL dialect. The different SQL dialects and language and database-specific access methods made the developer's life very difficult.

In the last ten years, two major advances have dramatically improved database access. First, most database systems have agreed on a common dialect of SQL known as SQL-92. While there are still variations (particularly with stored procedures), the database languages are almost uniform. Second, systems like ODBC have been developed, providing call-level interfaces where SQL statements are dynamically passed to the database and result sets are dynamically accessed.

Enter JDBC

So how does JDBC fit? Remember that Java is built on two underlying principles:

1. Platform independence. Code you write in Java should work on any hardware, any operating system, and, with JDBC, on any database. The intent is to provide a standard Java call-level interface for any database product.
2. Innovation within specifications. The JDBC specification provides a clear definition for what a vendor must build in order to support JDBC. The details of building the implementation are left up to the product vendors. This provides room for innovation and competition among vendors without sacrificing the primary goal of compatibility.

The JDBC specification provides a common interface for accessing database systems that should work across database platforms, regardless of differences in SQL or database structure. In practice, the second principle means that you must select a database driver developed by an outside vendor. Some of these drivers are free, and others are part of enterprise products such as application servers.

Moving past the selection of a database driver, JDBC offers a wide range of features for executing SQL statements and stored procedures. Enhancements with JDBC 2.0 include built-in support for connection pooling and resource management, bidirectional scrolling through SQL result sets, and a new system for actively editing data returned in an SQL result set.

Simple Application

The following code illustrates a simple application that connects to an ODBC database and performs a select statement on a table called trades.

```
import java.sql.*;
public class SimpleDBConnection {
public static void main(String[] args) {
```

```
  try {
    Class.forName("sun.jdbc.odbc.JdbcOdbcDriver");
    try {
      Connection conn = DriverManager.getConnection(
          "jdbc:odbc:dandelion", "sa", "password");
      Statement stmt = conn.createStatement();
      ResultSet rs = stmt.executeQuery("SELECT ticker,
          shares, price FROM trades");
      System.out.println("Ticker \t Shares \t
          Execution Price");
      while (rs.next()) {
        System.out.println(rs.getString("ticker") +
            "\t" + rs.getInt("shares") +
            "\t" + rs.getFloat("price"));
      }
      rs.close();
      stmt.close();
      conn.close();
    }
    catch (SQLException se) {
      System.out.println("SqlException: " + se.getMessage());
      se.printStackTrace(System.out);
    }
  }
  catch (ClassNotFoundException e) {
    System.out.println("ClassNotFound: " + e.getMessage());
  }
} //main
} //class
```

Listing 3.1 A simple JDBC example

Core Concepts

ARCHITECTURE

JDBC architecture is driven by the ideas of driver and database transparency. The JDBC specification contains interfaces that are implemented by the driver. Once the driver is registered with the `DriverManager` object, the client can work directly with `Connection`, `Statement`, and `ResultSet` objects.

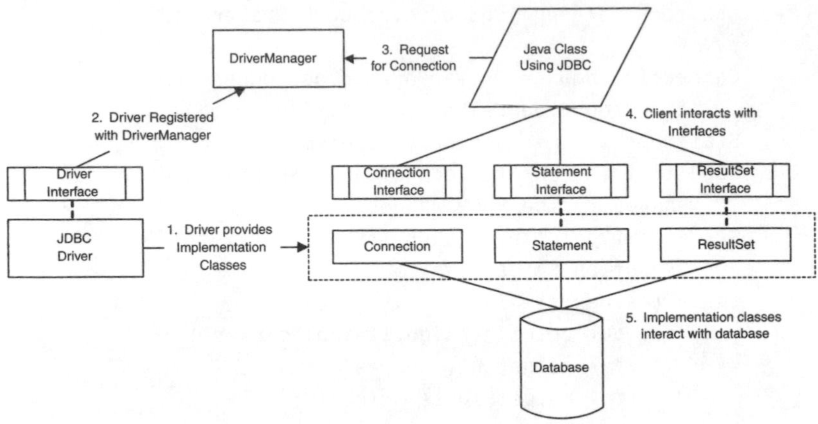

Figure 3.1 The developer works with simple Java objects. Behind the scenes, the DriverManager works with the driver to provide vendor-specific access to the database.

The client JDBC code is developed using the JDBC interfaces and the driver transparently communicates with the database. The developer never has to worry about database specific details.

Key Terminology

- Database—The whole point of JDBC is to provide a uniform connection between Java code and a database. The database might be anything from Microsoft Access to IBM's DB2.
- Driver—The driver is the core component for JDBC. Drivers are written by vendors and must support the basic features of the JDBC specification.
- `Connection`—A `Connection` is a Java interface defining a link to a database. The `Connection` is essentially a pipeline between your code and the database.
- `Statement`—A `Statement` is a Java interface that represents messages sent from your code to the database. These statements can use database-specific SQL or a form of SQL-92 that is compatible across all database systems. Newer, nonstandard SQL features are supported through special "escape sequences" that enable a programmer to switch database platforms without changing the SQL code.
- `ResultSet`—A `ResultSet` is a Java interface representing a set of data drawn from the database. Several kinds of SQL statements,

including stored procedures and SELECT statements, may return one or more `ResultSet` objects.

PACKAGES

The JDBC 2.0 implementation encompasses two packages of code:

- `java.sql`—The `java.sql` package contains the majority of class objects used for database access. The most important classes inside this package are the `DriverManager`, `Connection`, `SQLException`, `ResultSet`, `Statement`, `PreparedStatement`, and `CallableStatement`. Almost every database driver supports the components of this package.
- `javax.sql`—The `javax.sql` package is known as the JDBC Optional Package. This package adds support for connection pooling, interfaces to JNDI, and `RowSet`, which is a JavaBean extension of `ResultSet`. Database drivers are required to support this functionality for J2EE compliance.

SQL CONVENTIONS

Throughout this chapter, several standard conventions are used with SQL statements:

- All SQL-reserved words are capitalized (e.g., SELECT, INSERT, FROM, AND, WHERE).
- All table names and column names are entirely lowercase.

Some Special SQL: Escape Sequences

JDBC is designed to support the ANSI SQL-92 Entry Level specification. Almost every database implements this specification with the same syntax (e.g., SELECT, INSERT, DELETE). However, support and syntax for the next highest SQL specification, ANSI SQL-92 Selective Transitional Level, varies substantially. This specification includes outer joins and stored procedures. Because the syntax varies between databases, JDBC supports these features through an escape syntax that is identical to the escape syntax used with ODBC.

Each JDBC driver is responsible for translating this escape syntax into DBMS-specific syntax, assuming the underlying database supports the requested features. Eventually, when enough databases support

SQL-92 (one would hope this will happen as soon as SQL 1999 is completed), the escape syntax will become unnecessary.

The most commonly used components of the escape syntax are:

- Stored procedure calls:

```
{call sp_name[{{call sp_name[(argument1, argument2, ...)]}
```

or, where a procedure returns a result parameter:

```
{?= call sp_name[(argument1, argument2, ...)]}
```

- Dates:

```
SQL Date: {d 'yyyy-mm-dd'}
SQL Time: {t 'hh:mm:ss'}
SQL Timestamp: {ts 'yyyy-mm-dd hh:mm:ss.f...'}
  (f is fractional seconds)
```

- Scalar functions:

```
{fn [function(param1, param2)]}
e.g. {fn concat("fish", "heads")}
```

See java.sun.com/j2se/1.3/docs/guide/jdbc/spec/jdbc-spec.frame11.html for standard syntax of all supported scalar functions.

- Outer joins grammar:

```
{oj outer-join}
```

Where outer-join refers to:

```
table [left | right] OUTER JOIN {table | outer-join}
ON search-condition
```

For example, you might use SQL like this:

```
Statement stmt = conn.createStatement ();
ResultSet rset = stmt.executeQuery
  ("SELECT ename, dname
  FROM {OJ dept LEFT OUTER JOIN emp ON dept.deptno = emp.deptno}
  ORDER BY ename");
```

> Be warned however, that some drivers such as Sybase's and Oracle's, don't support this escape operation, and you may have to resort to sending vendor-specific SQL.

You can ignore the escape sequences and use vendor-specific SQL. However, if you change database vendors, you must evaluate every statement and recompile every class with the new syntax. If you plan on supporting multiple database vendors, you should use the escape syntax wherever possible.

Topic: Drivers and Connections

Implementing the most conceptually difficult part of a technology quite often involves the fewest lines of code. This is particularly true for JDBC. The topic of database drivers and establishing database `Connection` objects is, in the opinion of many Java developers, the most frustrating part of JDBC. However, loading a database driver and creating a `Connection` can be distilled into three key topics:

1. Installing the driver and setting the Java CLASSPATH.
2. Creating an instance of the driver.
3. Registering a `Connection` with a database using a database URL.

Once you have mastered these three areas, creating a database `Connection` can be as simple as a single line (or two) of code.

In this section, we will briefly cover the architecture and theory of database drivers and `Connections`. In addition, we will provide as many examples as possible of driver registration and database-specific URL patterns.

CORE CONCEPTS

Architecture

Creating a database `Connection` involves two simple steps. First, you must register the database driver with the `DriverManager`. Second, you must create a `Connection` to the specific database you require. Additional steps are performed behind the scenes to convert the `Connection` request into an actual database `Connection`.

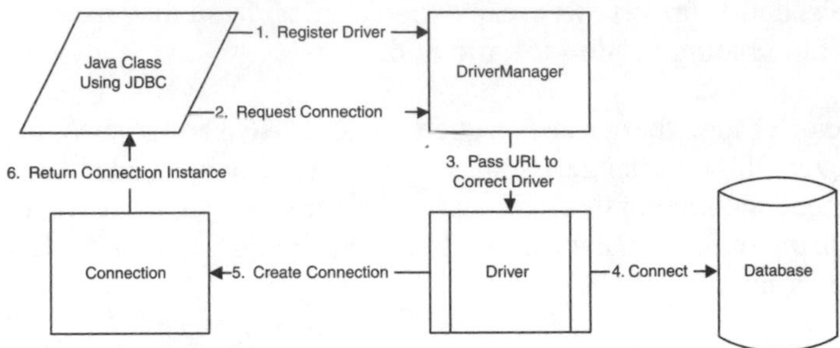

Figure 3.2 Registering a driver and creating a Connection is a multistep process. However, only the first two steps require actual code to implement. The remaining steps are handled by the DriverManager class and database driver.

Database Drivers

Most of the JDBC functionality you use consists of interfaces that are implemented in the database driver. Each driver vendor must implement the core features of JDBC, including `Connection`, `Statement`, and `ResultSet` objects. Additional features found in the `javax.sql module` are optional and may not be supported by the driver.

The JDBC specification defines four types of drivers. These definitions have implications with regard to speed and deployment. Understanding the driver types is not critical to using JDBC, but it can help you in selecting the correct driver for your application.

- Type 1: JDBC-ODBC bridge. This type of driver was developed as a temporary solution to help developers transition from ODBC to JDBC. As of this writing, JDBC drivers exist for all of the major databases, so you shouldn't ever need the JDBC-ODBC in a production system.
- Type 2: Native API, partly Java. These drivers use a Java bridge to connect to the native API of the database, and typically require a native shared library or DLL on all systems.
- Type 3: Net-Protocol, fully Java. These drivers use Java to communicate with the database and expose methods in a "net-friendly" way. Type 3 drivers do not require any client-side deployment.
- Type 4: Native Protocol, fully Java. Type 4 drivers are 100 percent Java drivers used primarily with thin Java clients or applets. These Drivers may require a minimal client-side installation.

All four types of drivers implement the same interfaces and provide the same functionality. However, choosing an appropriate driver type is the first step in choosing the correct driver.

Choosing a Driver

The standard J2EE installation comes with an experimental JDBC-ODBC bridge driver. You can certainly use this driver to get started. However, it is strongly recommended that you use an appropriate Java-based JDBC driver for any serious implementation effort.

So which driver is the best choice? It depends on what you are doing and what you can afford. Many JDBC drivers are free or come as part of other packages, such as application servers (e.g., WebLogic). Others are free for evaluation but require significant license fees after thirty days. The criteria for choosing a driver revolve around:

- Support for the required database(s). Is the driver designed to work with the database system(s) you expect to encounter?
- Driver type. The exact driver type is not generally a primary concern during development. Type 3 drivers are generally easier to deploy because they do not require additional client-side code.
- Support for the required feature(s). As of this writing, the official Sun JDBC driver list has over sixty drivers that support JDBC 2.0. However, this count does not differentiate between drivers that implement the basic specification and those that support the full specification. If you plan on using advanced features from the `javax.sql` package (`RowSet`, `DataSource`, etc.), make sure that the driver you choose supports them.
- Cost and support. How much will the driver cost, and how much support can you expect from the vendor? Will they help you with installation? Will you need to pay extra for maintenance and upgrades? Is the driver part of another package you already have or need to acquire, such as an EJB container or a JSP/Servlet engine?

Installing the Driver

Once you have found your driver, you will need to install it. Most drivers are JAR packages, so the actual installation is minimal: simply include the JAR package in your CLASSPATH environment variable. See Chapter 2 (Installation) for instructions on setting the CLASSPATH.

Registering the Driver

The next step is to register your driver with the `DriverManager`. The `DriverManager` is a container for all the registered drivers and a "super-factory" for `Connection` objects generated by the different drivers. Fortunately, the JDBC specification requires that all drivers self-register with the `DriverManager` as soon as the driver class has been instantiated.

There are three methods for registering a driver:

1. Explicitly instantiate a driver. This method is almost never used, as it requires you to explicitly define the driver in your code. If you switch drivers, you must modify your code and recompile. However, this method explains what the other methods are actually doing.

```
/** This example loads the jdbc-odbc bridge Driver that is part of
j2ee.  Other Drivers will have different class names. **/
sun.jdbc.odbc.JdbcOdbcDriver myDriver =
  new sun.jdbc.odbc.JdbcOdbcDriver();
DriverManager.registerDriver(myDriver);
```

Listing 3.2 Loading a driver

2. Include the driver in jdbc.drivers property. You can put the driver name in the jdbc.drives property at run time using the "-D" directive:

```
java –Djdbc.drivers=DriverName ProgramName
```

   Notice that there should not be a space between -D and the driver name. This directive forces the virtual machine to instantiate an instance of the specified driver, which will automatically register the driver with the DriverManager. The main drawback of this method is that you must remember to use the -D setting every time you run the program.
3. Use the `Class.forName()` method. The third and most common method is to load the class into memory using the `Class.forName()` technique. This line of code uses the Java ClassLoader to search the CLASSPATH and load the driver's class file by name. The driver class has a static initializer that automatically calls

```
DriverManager.registerDriver().
```

```
/**This may throw a ClassNotFoundException!
The call is Class.forName("Driver.name") **/
Class.forName("COM.Cloudscape.core.JDBCDriver");
```

This method has the advantage of using a simple `String` to name the driver. The `String` can be easily incorporated into a shared `java.util.Properties` object, based on a configuration file for your project. In other words, your code doesn't need to know the name of the driver until runtime, and you do not need to worry about a system-level property setting.

Connection Object

The next step in connecting to a database is to create a JDBC `Connection` object. This acts as a factory for `Statement` objects that give you the ability to submit SQL commands to the database. Creating a `Connection` involves a single call to the `DriverManager`. Requesting a `Connection` object follows the form:

```
Connection conn = DriverManager.getConnection("DatabaseURL",
    "username", "password");
```

The `getConnection()` method is overloaded to accept a `java.util.Properties` file instead of a username and password. It can also accept a URL that encodes the username and password.

Remember that the `DriverManager` is a container for all of the registered drivers. In order to get the correct `Connection` object, you need to tell the `DriverManager` which driver it should use and to which database it should connect. This information is encapsulated in a Database URL.

Database URLs

A Database Uniform Resource Locator (URL) generally follows the form

```
jdbc:Drivername:datasource
```

This format is very loosely defined, and each driver can use a different format for the URL. However, every URL will start with "jdbc:", identify the driver either fully or with a short name, and identify the datasource. The datasource may be a database name, a TNSNames entry (for Oracle), an ODBC data source (for JDBC-ODBC bridge), or some other string that includes sufficient information to connect to the database. These URL formats are driver-specific, which generally means they are also database-specific. Several common URL formats are illustrated in the Examples section.

Connection Pooling

A connection pool is a collection of premade `Connection` objects. Rather than asking the `DriverManager` for a new `Connection`, you ask the connection pool. Because the pool maintains a set of active `Connection` objects, you can save the overhead of creating a new one each time you need to communicate with the database. Connection pools are generally implemented in extended JDBC drivers (e.g., JDBC Broker), or as the `javax.sql.DataSource` interface. In the first case, the connection pool is built into the driver, and the code required to configure the pool will be vendor-specific. In the second case, you will need to configure the `DataSource`. This configuration is also vendor-specific, but generally involves the following settings:

- Driver name, JDBC URL, user name, and password. The `DataSource` will take care of loading the driver and connecting to the database.
- Pool size. Initial and maximum capacity, growth rate, and shrinkage rate properties configure the pool size.
- JNDI name. `DataSource` objects are always accessed via a naming service.

In your code, you can use JNDI (Chapter 4) to connect to a `DataSource`.

```
/**In this example, the datasource is stored in the J2EE server
environment context **/
String dbURL = "java:comp/env/jdbc/AccountDB";
InitialContext ic = new InitialContext();
DataSource ds = (DataSource) ic.lookup(dbUrl);
Connection myConn = ds.getConnection();
//work with connection
myConn.close();
```

Listing 3.3 Using a connection pool

To hand a `Connection` back to the pool, simply use the `close()` method as if it were a normal `Connection`.

EXAMPLES

Registering Drivers

Remember that drivers are generally JARs, so the naming convention usually follows the form *company.name.Drivertype.Drivername,* although this is not a standard. The following are examples of some common driver names that you could use with `Class.forName()` or by setting the jdbc.Drivers property.

- JDBC-ODBC bridge—`sun.jdbc.odbc.JdbcOdbcDriver`
- Cloudscape driver—`COM.Cloudscape.core.JDBCDriver` (part of J2EE installation)
- Lotus Notes driver—`fr.dyade.mediation.jdbc.LotusNotes`
- Sybase driver—`com.sybase.jdbc2.jdbc.SybDriver`
- Oracle driver—`oracle.jdbc.driver.OracleDriver`

Database URLs

The following examples illustrate common URL formats for different drivers.

- Oracle JDBC ThinDriver jdbc:oracle:thin:@*hostname:port :database.* The default Oracle port is 1521.
- Oracle Type 2 driver (uses Oracle's TNSNames entry)—jdbc :oracle:oci8:@*SQLNETinstanceName* (e.g., jdbc:oracle:oci8:@CodeNotes)
- JDBC-ODBC bridge (uses an ODBC datasource you must establish on your machine)—jdbc:odbc:*datasource;param=value;* (e.g., jdbc:odbc:CodeNotes;uid=sa;pwd="snuffelupugus")
- Cloudscape driver—jdbc:cloudscape:*databaseName;attributes*
- Lotus Notes driver—jdbc:notes:*databasefile.nsf[+additional files]* (e.g., jdbc:notes:mydata.nsf+yourdata.nsf)
- Sybase—jdbc:sybase:Tds:*ipaddress:port:database.* The default port is 4100.

HOW AND WHY

How Do I Find Out if a Connection Is Still Open and Alive?

Generally, your first indication that a connection may be dead is that an `SQLException` is thrown in a place where you don't expect it. The `Connection` object does have an `isOpen()` method, but this method only tells you whether the `close()` method has been called. If you really need to know whether your `Connection` is valid, it is often best to send a small test statement to the database and verify the result. However, if you have designed your code to handle SQLExceptions, then you should not need to test explicitly for a valid Connection.

Why Does My Code Keep Throwing ClassNotFoundException?

If you are using the Class.forName() syntax to register the driver, you may encounter the ClassNotFoundException. This exception is thrown when the class loader cannot find the database driver. Check your CLASSPATH environment variable and make sure that the driver package (usually a .jar file) is listed.

How Do I Find the Newest Driver for My Database?

The best place to start looking for driver information is the Java Driver Database website: http://industry.java.sun.com/products/jdbc/drivers. Sun makes a significant effort to update this driver database, and most vendors take advantage of the free advertising and register their drivers here.

Why Should I Use Connection Pooling Rather Than Managing My Own Connections?

Creating, opening, and closing a Connection involves a small but significant amount of overhead in both time and memory. Using connection pooling provides several advantages. First, the Connection objects are already established and waiting for use. This reduces the time and memory overhead for creating a new Connection each time you want to perform a database call. Second, an outside system handles the life cycle of the Connection, including creating, closing, and generating new connections. This means you can devote more time to your specific task and less time to the husbandry of connecting to a database. Third, fully developed connection pooling is often provided as a feature with EJB platforms such as BEA WebLogic and some JDBC 2.0 Type 3 drivers that support javax.sql.ConnectionPoolDataSource (e.g., Merant's DataDirect; www.merant.com). These features can save you considerable time and effort in the development of your classes.

BUGS AND CAVEATS

Managing Connections

Remember to close your Connection objects! If you don't close your Connection, you may tie up all of the database Connection resources, in which case you must restart your database or, at least, kill the connections through a database admin tool. Although it is rather rare, it is possible to crash a database by setting the database connection timeout high and creating many open `Connection` objects. The typical symptom of this problem is an unexpected `SQLException` that reports a failure to create a new `Connection`.

Connection Pooling

Remember to release your `Connection` objects back to the pool using `Connection.close()` as soon as you are finished with them. If you do not explicitly release your `Connection`, most connection pooling systems will not return it to the pool until the timeout has passed. You may be unable to grab a new `Connection` because some of the pool connections will be allocated to dead objects and won't have timed out yet.

DESIGN NOTES

Error Trapping

How and where should you handle error trapping for creating connections? When using connection pools, it is common to use the following pattern:

```
public class DatabaseOperationProcessor {
public void execute(DatabaseOperation databaseOp) {
  /** Aquire a javax.sql.DataSource, and place in variable
     dataSource. **/
  Connection connection = null;
  Statement statement = null;
  try {
    connection = dataSource.getConnection();
    /** insert your code here to create statement
    object and perform work. **/
  } catch (SQLException e) {
    // Perform error handling or re-throw exception
  } finally {
    try {
      if (statement != null) statement.close();
      if (connection != null) connection.close();
    } catch (Exception e) {
      /** Exceptions are rarely caught here
      because close() is a very clean operation **/
    } //try
```

```
  } //finally
}//execute
}//class
```

Listing 3.4 A generic pattern for connection pools

If anything goes wrong, this pattern guarantees that the statement is closed (hence freeing the underlying cursor—no "Oracle has run out of cursors" errors), and the `Connection` is closed or released back to the pool. Notice that the `finally` block checks to ensure that the `Statement` and `Connection` actually exist before attempting the `close()` method.

SUMMARY

There are two steps in registering a database driver and connecting to a database. These steps generally require two lines of code.

1. Register the database driver. The most common method is to use `Class.forName()` to instantiate and register the driver programmatically.

```
Class.forName("my.Driver.classname");
```

2. Create a `Connection` to your database. Remember that the only challenge here is determining the correct URL. URL formats are driver-specific.

```
Connection conn = DriverManager.getConnection(
    "my.database.url","username", "password");
```

Finally, remember to close your `Connection` when you are finished with it, whether you are creating a `Connection` manually or using connection pooling.

In the following sections, we will use a `Connection` object to execute SQL statements, extract metadata about a database, and execute stored procedures.

Topic: Statements

Now that you've made it through the sometimes confusing task of establishing a `Connection`, what can you do with it? How do you submit statements to a database and receive the results? This chapter explains how to use the various types of `Statement` objects, which allow you to communicate meaningfully with a database.

Almost all databases are built on some derivative of the SQL-92 standard. This standard provides a common language for accessing data in a database. The JDBC `Statement` objects provide the pipeline for transmitting SQL to the database and receiving data. A `Statement` is simply an abstraction of an SQL statement. There are three types of abstractions that represent the different kinds of SQL statements: dynamic (`Statement`), reusable (`PreparedStatement`), and stored procedures (`CallableStatement`).

CORE CONCEPTS

The JDBC standard provides for three basic types of statements: `Statement`, `PreparedStatement`, and `CallableStatement`. Each interface has a different purpose (detailed in the next sections), although all three can be used for issuing SQL directives to a database.

Statement

The basic `Statement` object is the parent class for the other two `Statement` types. This interface allows you to submit basic SQL to the database and retrieve `ResultSet` objects.

```
Statement stmt = conn.createStatement();
ResultSet rs = stmt.executeQuery( "SELECT * FROM stocks");
```

To create a `Statement`, you need a valid `Connection`. Then you can use the `Connection` as a factory to generate new statements using the `createStatement()` method. Once you have a valid `Statement` object, you can use `execute()`, `executeQuery()`, or `executeUpdate()` to perform SQL actions. All of these methods are explained in detail later in this section.

PreparedStatement

In some cases, you will want to reuse an SQL statement. The `PreparedStatement` interface extends the `Statement` interface by generating a precompiled SQL statement that you can reuse. Because it is precompiled on the database, it will run faster for repeated calls. The disadvantage is that each `PreparedStatement` is locked into a single, specific SQL command.

Using the Statement method, you generate the SQL on the fly. With a PreparedStatement, on the other hand, you create the SQL and then insert the values as a second step.

```
//Create the statement
String mySQL = "INSERT INTO stocks (ticker, last_bid ) " +
  VALUES (?, ?)";
PreparedStatement prepStmt = conn.prepareStatement(mySQL);
//Insert the values to replace the ? placeholders
prepStmt.clearParameters();
prepStmt.setString(1, "MSFT");
prepStmt.setFloat(2, 60.5);
/**Use executeUpdate() since this is an INSERT statement rowCount
will hold the number of rows added, which should be 1 **/
int rowCount = prepStmt.executeUpdate();
```

Listing 3.5 Using a PreparedStatement

When you generate a PreparedStatement, you use the Connection object as a factory and pass in the SQL statement. The SQL statement looks just like regular SQL, except that you replace key input (IN) elements with a "?" placeholder. These are some examples of ways you can use a "?" placeholder.

- Comparison values—"WHERE id = ?"
- Between statements—"WHERE id BETWEEN ? AND ?"
- Insert values—"INSERT INTO stocks (ticker, last_bid) VALUES(?, ?)"
- Update values—"UPDATE stocks SET last_bid = ? WHERE ticker = ?"

There are commands for each of the datatypes, although most commonly you will need setString(), setInt(), setFloat(), or setDate(). The common methods all work by passing in two arguments: the first is the index of the input value, and the second is the value. Input arguments are always numbered from left to right, starting with 1. Some special case setXXXX() methods use additional arguments for formatting. For example, the setDate() method allows you to set the date by passing in a java.util.Calendar in addition to the date value.

In the earlier example, the SQL statement was:

```
String mySQL = "INSERT INTO stocks (ticker, last_bid )
  VALUES (?, ?)";
```

The first parameter is a varchar, which maps to a `String` in Java. The second parameter is a `Float`, so the code to fill the statement is:

```
prepStmt.clearParameters();
prepStmt.setString(1, "MSFT");
prepStmt.setFloat(2, 60.5);
```

Since we can reuse the statement, we always want to make sure to use the `clearParameters()` method to remove any old data.

ExecuteUpdate vs ExecuteQuery vs Execute

Depending upon what type of SQL you want to execute, you will generally need to use the `executeUpdate()` or `executeQuery()` methods. In cases where your SQL may return multiple `ResultSets`, or when you do not know the actual SQL command at compile-time, you can use the `Execute()` method, which supports both queries and updates.

ExecuteUpdate

The `executeUpdate()` command is used for SQL statements that do not directly return data from the database. This includes UPDATE, DELETE, INSERT, and ALTER statements. The `executeUpdate()` method will typically return an integer indicating the number of rows affected for UPDATE, DELETE, and INSERT commands. For other SQL statements, the `executeUpdate()` method returns a value of 0 for successful execution, although you should use the `getWarnings()` method to check for any nonfatal exceptions.

ExecuteQuery

If you are requesting data from the database, or expect data to be returned by your statement, you need to use `executeQuery()`. This method is used almost exclusively for SELECT statements or calls to stored procedures that have fixed arguments. The return value is always a `ResultSet` object.

Execute

The `execute()` command is a generic method for executing SQL of unknown type. You should use this method when you don't know whether the SQL will return a `ResultSet` or not. The `execute()` method returns a `boolean` value, true if a `ResultSet` was returned and false if an update count is waiting.

In order to access the data returned from an `execute()` command, you must use the `getResultSet()` or `getUpdateCount()` command. The following code fragment illustrates how this works:

```
/** assume we built a Statement called stmt and then executed some
SQL of unknown type.  It could be either a Query or an Update **/
boolean rsCheck = stmt.execute(sqlString);
/**if rsCheck is true, then it's a Query, otherwise it was an
update**/
if (rsCheck) {
  /**The ResultSet is waiting in the Statement and we need to
  use getResultSet to extract it. **/
  ResultSet rs1 = stmt.getResultSet();
} else {
  /**The SQL was an Update, so we need to use getUpdateCount to
  find out how many rows were affected.  Remember that for some
  types of queries getUpdateCount will always be 0 **/
  int rowCount = stmt.getUpdateCount();
}
```

Listing 3.6 Using the Execute() method

In some cases, certain SQL may generate multiple `ResultSet` objects. You can extract multiple `ResultSets` using the `getMoreResults()` method, although the exact details are covered in the website CN `J2030001`.

Recap

Method	SQL Commands	Return Values
executeUpdate	UPDATE, DELETE, INSERT	Number of rows affected by statement.
executeUpdate	ALTER, EXEC, other methods that do not return results	These statements always return an integer value of 0. After all, no rows were updated by the query.
executeQuery	SELECT	ResultSet object containing the results of the query.
execute	Any	True if a ResultSet is waiting, False if an updatecount is waiting.

Table 3.1 Each Execute method accepts different types of SQL and returns different values. Choose the most appropriate method for your SQL statement.

So why not just use `execute()` all the time? The `execute()` method is generally slower than the other methods and involves more lines of code to extract your data. If the SQL is hard-coded in your class, or is always either a query or an update, why not use the correct method and save both time and typing?

ResultSet

When you use the `executeQuery()` method or `execute()` and `getResultSet()`, the `Statement` generates a `ResultSet` as the return value. `ResultSets` are fully described in the ResultSet topic later in this chapter. For our current purposes, think of a `ResultSet` as a table of values that have been extracted from the database.

CallableStatement

One of the difficulties in creating an API that works with different database systems is that the syntax for stored procedures is often very different from system to system. In fact, the stored procedure language has always been one of the most contentious issues in standardizing SQL. The JDBC specification accounts for this problem by defining a standard call structure and requiring that the database driver perform the translation to the database specific call.

The `CallableStatement` interface extends the `PreparedStatement` interface with features specific to the handling of stored procedures. `CallableStatement` is very similar to `PreparedStatement` in that you replace input (IN) and output (OUT) values with a "?" character.

```
/**Assume we have a stored procedure with this declaration:
get_name(in varchar username, out varchar fullName) **/
String mySQL = "{call get_name(?,?)}";
CallableStatement callStmt =
    conn.prepareCall(mySQL);
callStmt.setString(1, "lbrillo");
callStmt.registerOutParameter(2,
    Types.STRING);
callStmt.execute();
String myOut = callStmt.getString(2);
/**Note that we extract the second parameter.  Parameters are
numbered from left to right, regardless of whether they are in, out
or inout **/
```

Listing 3.7 Using the CallableStatement

The basic syntax for a stored procedure call depends on whether the stored procedure returns an output value. Some databases do not support output values, so this syntax may be database-dependent. The two formats are:

- No return value: {call *stored_procedure_name*[(?[,?])]}
  examples: "{call *refresh_tables*}"
  "{call *get_user_id*(?,?)}"
- Return value: {? = call *stored_procedure_name*[(?[,?])]}
  examples: "{? = call get_next_id_sequence}"
  "{? = call get_user_name(?)}"

Once you have prepared the correct escape sequence, use the `prepareCall()` function of the `Connection` object to generate the `CallableStatement`.

`CallableStatement` objects may use input and/or output parameters. Generally, input parameters are set using the same `setXXXX()` methods used for a `PreparedStatement`. Output parameters must be registered using `registerOutParameter()` before the statement is executed, and then the return values can be accessed using `getXXXX()` methods. There are a few key points to consider when working with IN and OUT parameters:

- All parameters are numbered from left to right, starting with 1. In a stored procedure that has a return value, the return value is number 1 and the first IN parameter is number 2.
- Input parameters are set the same way as for a `PreparedStatement`. Use the appropriate `setXXXX()` method for the datatype, then pass in the parameter number and the value.
- `RegisterOutParameter()` requires a parameter number and a `java.sql.Types` data type identifier. These types are formatted as `Types.FLOAT`, `Types.STRING`, `Types.INTEGER`, etc.

Once you have passed in all IN parameters and registered all OUT parameters, you will be able to execute the statement using the `execute()` command. After execution, you can access the results using `getXXXX()` methods. The `getXXXX()` methods are data-type-specific and require the parameter number.

EXAMPLES

The following examples illustrate common uses for each type of statement. Each example assumes that you have successfully created a `Connection` object called `dbConnection`.

Statement

This first example illustrates the use of the `Statement` object to perform a simple SQL statement.

```
/**It's generally better form to prepare your statement in a String
outside of the execute call.  That way you can easily print it to
the screen for debugging. **/
String mySQL = "SELECT ticker, last_bid FROM stocks";
try {
  //Create the statement
  Statement stmt =
  dbConnection.prepareStatement(mySQL);
  //Execute the query
  ResultSet rs = stmt.executeQuery(mySQL);
  /**At this point, we can process our result
  set.  For now, just dump to the screen **/
  while (rs.next()) {
    System.out.println(
        rs.getString("ticker") + "\t"
        + rs.getFloat("last_bid"));
  }
  //Close the ResultSet and Statement
  rs.close();
  stmt.close();
} catch (SQLException e) {
  System.out.println("Error! The SQL was: "
      + mySQL);
  System.out.println("The error is:  " +
      e.getMessage());
  e.printStackTrace(out);
} //catch
```

Listing 3.8 Statement example

PreparedStatement

This example illustrates the use of a `PreparedStatement` to perform a series of INSERT statements. You should use a `PreparedStatement` when you need to use the same SQL repeatedly.

```
String mySQL = "INSERT INTO stocks (ticker, last_bid)
  VALUES (?,?)";
try {
  //Create the statement
```

```
  PreparedStatement pStmt =
      dbConnection.prepareStatement(mySQL);
  /**We create a small array of values for this example.
  Usually, you will draw values from a data file or outside
  source, such as an array passed into your method **/
  String[] tickers = new String[] {"SUNW","MSFT", "IBM", "ORCL"};
  float[] last_bid = new float[] {20.71f, 68.04f, 114.47f, 20.31f};
  /**build loop for the statement
  for (int i = 0; i < tickers.length; i++) {
    //clear the previous values
    pStmt.clearParameters();
    //setting the parameters
    pStmt.setString(1, tickers[i]);
    pStmt.setFloat(2, last_bid[i]);
    //execute the statement
    pStmt.executeUpdate();
  } //for
  //close the statement
  pStmt.close();
} //try
//Catch block removed.  See previous example.
```

Listing 3.9 PreparedStatement example

CallableStatement

This example executes an Oracle stored procedure. Note that JDBC does not include a type mapping to return a `ResultSet` cursor from an OUT parameter or as a function return type. We need to use the Oracle-specific driver call to perform this operation. The first listing is an SQL script for creating the table and the stored procedure.

```
CREATE TABLE products (
    product_id    INTEGER,
    product_name  VARCHAR2(50),
    creation_date DATE);
INSERT INTO products VALUES (1, 'Product 1',
        TO_DATE('1975-01-05', 'YYYY-MM-DD'));
INSERT INTO products VALUES (2, 'Product 2',
        TO_DATE(' '1983-05-01', 'YYYY-MM-DD'));
CREATE OR REPLACE PACKAGE cursor_types
  AS TYPE cursor_ref REF CURSOR;
END;
```

```
CREATE OR REPLACE FUNCTION get_products_created_after
    (afterDate IN DATE) RETURN
cursor_types.cursor_ref IS productResults cursor_types.cursor_ref;
BEGIN
    open productResults FOR SELECT * FROM products p
        WHERE p.creation_date > afterDate;
    RETURN (productResults);
END get_products_created_after;
```

Listing 3.10a Setup for the CallableStatement example

The following Java code would be used to execute the "get_products_created_after" procedure.

```
// Assume conn is valid connection object
CallableStatement queryStatement = conn.prepareCall(
  "{call get_products_created_after(?, ?)}");
queryStatement.registerOutParameter(1,
  oracle.jdbc.driver.OracleTypes.CURSOR);
java.util.GregorianCalendar desiredDate =
  new java.util.GregorianCalendar(1980, 1, 1);
queryStatement.setDate(2,
  new java.sql.Date( desiredDate.getTime().getTime() ) );
queryStatement.execute();
ResultSet rs = ((oracle.jdbc.driver.OracleCallableStatement)
  stmt).getCursor(1);
while (rs.next()) {
  // Display objects.
}
rs.close()
queryStatement.close();
```

Listing 3.10b The CallableStatement example

HOW AND WHY

How Do I Use a Stored Procedure with INOUT Parameters?

In the earlier section on `CallableStatements`, both IN (input) and OUT (output) parameters were demonstrated. A third type of parameter is both input and output (INOUT). When your database and drivers support INOUT parameters, you can use them by "overloading" a parameter with both a `setXXXX()` method and a registerOutParameter method. For example:

```
//my_stored_proc has a single INOUT parameter.
String mySQL = "{call my_stored_proc(?)}";
CallableStatement callStmt = conn.prepareCall(mySQL);
callStmt.setString(1, "This is an IN");
callStmt.registerOutParameter(1, Types.STRING);
callStmt.execute();
String myOut = cstmt.getString(1);
```

Listing 3.11 Using a stored procedure with INOUT parameters

BUGS AND CAVEATS

FetchSize and FetchDirection

The `Statement` object has two properties that are used by the driver to optimize the query. The first property is `fetchSize()`, which is the number of rows that should be fetched into memory. The second property is `fetchDirection()`. If you know you will be iterating through a `ResultSet` in a particular direction (FETCH_FORWARD or FETCH_BACKWARD), you can use `fetchDirection()` to tell the driver to grab the rows in a preferred order.

However, both of these properties are merely suggestions. The driver may choose to ignore your suggestions and retrieve the rows with a different `fetchSize`, or in a different `fetchDirection`.

Multiple ResultSets

Remember that a `ResultSet` is an open database cursor. You can only have one open `ResultSet` per `Statement` object. If you intend to reuse the `Statement`, you must first close the `ResultSet`. In fact, many drivers will not allow two open `ResultSet` objects on a single `Connection`.

If you encounter a situation where having two `ResultSet` objects would be useful, either store the content of the first `ResultSet` in memory as a `list`, `vector`, or `array` and then generate the second `ResultSet`, or convert your code to a stored procedure.

DESIGN NOTES

Error Trapping

Every JDBC method that contacts the database throws `SQLException`. Depending on your JDBC driver, the `SQLException.getMessage()` function will usually provide you with the actual error as reported by the database. However, this may not be that helpful, as many database vendors provide obscure error messages. `SQLException.printStackTrace()` may also be helpful in determining the location of the error, but it does not generally display the actual database error messages. Some common exception causes are:

- Bad SQL statements. If possible, always print the SQL statement in your exception message. Badly formed SQL is a very common cause of `SQLExceptions`. Quite often, simple inspection of the statement will identify the problem, although you may want to try executing the statement with an external SQL tool such as Embarcadero, ISQL, SQLplus, SQL Navigator, or SQL Worksheet.
- Premature termination of a `Connection`, `Statement`, or `ResultSet`. If you close the `Connection` before processing your `ResultSet`, you will often generate `SQLExceptions`. Make sure that you keep the `Connection` and `Statement` open until you have finished with the `ResultSet`. This order of operations is discussed in greater detail in the `ResultSet` topic.
- Firewalls. Some firewalls have a nasty habit of closing communication ports that have been "idle" for too long. This can sometimes cause problems if you have a `Connection`, `Statement`, or `ResultSet` that you need to keep active for an extended period. This problem can generally be resolved by working with the firewall administrator to resolve port administration.

java.sql.SQLWarning

In addition to SQL errors that throw `SQLExceptions`, a database will automatically take care of some problems, such as minor data-type conversions or truncations. These errors generate `SQLWarning` messages, which are not sufficiently critical to throw an exception. Each `Statement` and `ResultSet` builds up a stack of `SQLWarnings` that you can access with the `getWarnings()` and `getNextWarning()` methods.

```
String mySQL = "INSERT INTO contacts (name, address1, address2,
  city, state) values ("JoJo", "123 Main St", "", "Whoville",
  "Who");
Statement stmt = conn.createStatement();
stmt.executeUpdate(mySQL);
SQLWarning w = stmt.getWarnings();
while (w != null) {
```

```
    System.out.println(SQLWarning: " + w.getMessage());
    w = stmt.getNextWarning();
}
```

Listing 3.12 SQLWarnings

These warnings may have a significant impact on your data, and you should generally check for warnings on INSERT statements.

Basic Patterns

JDBC operations can usually be reduced to a simple pattern of boilerplate code. The steps are:

1. Create the `Connection`, or get one from a pool.
2. Create `Statement`, `PreparedStatement`, or `CallableStatement`.
3. Do the work (execute statement, process results).
4. Handle any exceptions.
5. Close the `Statement` and `Connection` (in a `finally` block).

The CodeNotes website has several template classes that follow this pattern CN J2030002.

SUMMARY

`Statement` objects are created from the `Connection` object. There are three types of statements (`Statement`, `PreparedStatement`, and `CallableStatement`), each with a specific purpose. Use the statement that most closely matches your needs.

Each `Statement` has three execution methods: `execute()`, `executeQuery()`, and `executeUpdate()`. Use the method that most closely matches your needs.

Topic: ResultSets

Every type of database connectivity system has some form of formatted output that results from a SELECT statement or a call to a stored procedure. In JDBC, the `ResultSet` fills this primary need. This section will show you how to perform basic operations on a `ResultSet`.

The basic `ResultSet` was introduced with the first JDBC specification. In JDBC 1.0, a `ResultSet` was a very simple, one-pass, forward-only cursor. The JDBC 2.0 specification extended the `ResultSet` to allow for forward and reverse scrolling as well as direct access to any row. Features for in-place editing and insertion of new rows were also added, making `ResultSet` a very powerful tool for handling database data. However, the new features come at the price of opening up greater potential for database conflicts, stale data, and conflicts over read/write access.

CORE CONCEPTS

The ResultSet object

As discussed in the Statement topic above, a `ResultSet` is returned when you use the `executeQuery()` method, and may be returned using the `getResultSet()` method. The `ResultSet` object provides access to the data that you have extracted from the database.

ResultSet Iteration

The most basic form of navigation through a `ResultSet` involves reading one row at a time, from the first row to the last. This type of one-pass forward iteration is built into the `ResultSet` object using the `next()` function. A `ResultSet` initially points to "before the first row," so you always must use `next()` to access data. The `next()` method attempts to iterate to the next row in the `ResultSet` and returns `false` if the end of the `ResultSet` was encountered.

The following code fragment illustrates a very common case for using a `ResultSet`:

```
//This code assumes you have a ResultSet called rs
while (rs.next()) {
  //extract data and process it
}
```

The JDBC 2.0 specification added iteration methods that essentially provide random access to the `ResultSet`. These methods allow you to move backward and jump around inside a `ResultSet`.

- `absolute(int row)` moves to specified row number
- `relative(int rows)` moves "rows" forward (positive integer) or backward (negative integer) from the current position
- `previous()` moves back one row, equivalent to `relative(-1)`
- `first()` moves to the first row, equivalent to `beforeFirst()` followed by `next()`

- `last()` moves to the last row, equivalent to `afterLast()` followed by `previous()`
- `afterLast()` moves to the end of the `ResultSet`. The `getXXXX()` and `updateXXXX()` methods will fail unless you iterate to a valid position.
- `beforeFirst()` moves to the beginning of the `ResultSet`. The `getXXXX()` and `updateXXXX()` methods will fail unless you iterate to a valid position. This is the state of a brand-new `ResultSet`.

In order to take advantage of these methods, you must modify the way you create your original `Statement` object. The following code fragment illustrates how to create a scrollable `ResultSet` from a valid `Connection` object called `dbConnection`.

```
Statement stmt = dbConnection.createStatement(
   ResultSet.TYPE_SCROLL_INSENSITIVE, ResultSet.CONCUR_READ_ONLY);
ResultSet rs = stmt.executeQuery(mySQL);
```

Listing 3.13 Building a scrollable ResultSet

There are actually three options for scrollable `ResultSet` objects. The first option (`ResultSet.TYPE_FORWARD_ONLY`) is the default setting, which allows a single forward-only pass through the `ResultSet`. The second option (`ResultSet.TYPE_SCROLL_INSENSITIVE`), illustrated above, is a "Dirty Read" and is insensitive to changes made to the data; you are creating a snapshot of the data that will not be updated if the underlying data changes in the database. The third option is to use `ResultSet.TYPE_SCROLL_SENSITIVE`, which will recognize changes in the underlying data. These terms relate to a core database concept called isolation. For a more thorough description of isolation, see the website CN J2030006.

Extracting Data

Whether you are using basic iteration or a scrollable `ResultSet`, finding the row you need is only the first step. The `ResultSet` object has `getXXXX()` methods for all Java data types. The database driver tries to translate the SQL data type to the requested Java data type.

Each of these methods is overloaded to accept either a column index or a column name. Columns are numbered from left to right, and the first column is always number 1. If you use column names, the name is case-insensitive, regardless of the underlying database. These methods are illustrated in the following code fragment (which assumes a valid `Connection` object, called `dbConnection`):

```
String mySQL = "SELECT stock, shares FROM portfolio WHERE id = 3";
Statement stmt = dbConnection.prepareStatement(mySQL);
ResultSet rs = stmt.executeQuery(mySQL);
//This method will return the value from the first column
String stock = rs.getString(1);
//This method will return the 'shares' column
int shares = rs.getInt("shares");
```

Listing 3.14 Data extraction from a ResultSet

Generally, you should use the column name version only when your SQL call explicitly names the returned data columns. If you do not know the SQL until runtime, or if it changes frequently, you will be better off using the column number version and a `ResultSetMetaData` object to extract the names.

ResultSetMetaData

So what do you do when the SQL is passed into your class object and you don't know how many columns are returned, what datatypes they are, or even what the column names are? When you use a "SELECT * FROM" type of SQL command, for instance, you may not necessarily know what columns are returned.

The JDBC specification includes a `ResultSetMetaData` object that can be used to find out the number of columns, the name of each column, and the data type of the column. The following example displays the results from a `ResultSet` in a simple table:

```
/**This example assumes you have a valid ResultSet called rs.
Error trapping and the various close() statements have been
omitted. First, we create the ResultSetMetaData object **/
ResultSetMetaData meta = rs.getMetaData();
//next, we loop through the MetaData, creating a header row
int numberOfColumns = meta.getColumnCount();
for (int colNumber=1; colNumber<=numberOfColumns; colNumber++) {
  System.out.print(meta.getTableName(colNumber) + "."
    + meta.getColumnLabel(colNumber));
  System.out.print(meta.getColumnTypeName(colNumber));
  //put a tab between names unless it's the last column
  if (colNumber < numberOfColumns)
    System.out.print("/t");
} //for
System.out.println();
```

```
//loop through and display the results as Strings.
while(rs.next()) {
  for (int colNumber=1; colNumber<=numberOfColumns; colNumber++) {
    System.out.print(rs.getString(colNumber));
    if (colNumber < numberOfColumns)
      System.out.print("\t");
  } //for
  System.out.println(); //line break
} //while
```

Listing 3.15 Using ResultSetMetaData

Unfortunately, as you can see in the example, knowing the data type doesn't help you extract or process the data. The common solutions to this problem are to convert every data type to a String or to build a very large "switch" statement handling each of the possible data types differently CN J2030003.

Managing Resources

A ResultSet is always tied to a Statement, which is always tied to a Connection. All three objects require resources on the client and the database. Database resources include connections, cursors, and locks, while a temporary memory cache is required on the client. While each driver and database manages resources in its own way, every JDBC developer must understand when and how to explicitly close a ResultSet, Statement, or Connection.

A Connection is the actual pipeline to the database. Once a Connection is closed, no further actions can be taken until the Connection has been reestablished. A Statement is an abstraction of a database query. The Statement provides the context and maintains the database-side resources for the ResultSet. When the parent Statement has been closed, the ResultSet can no longer communicate with the database.

The ResultSet holds some amount of data in a local memory cache. The cache may contain the complete set of results or a partial set. If the cache is partial, the ResultSet will automatically requery the database for the next set of data when you ask for it (by iterating to the next row). This process happens transparently. Your JDBC code acts as if all the data is available locally.

In order to avoid problems with resource management, you should strive to perform "surgical strikes" against the database. Issue your statement, then immediately process the ResultSet and release the Connection. The longer you hold a Connection, Statement, or ResultSet open, the greater the chance for problems.

The general order of JDBC operations should be:

1. Create the `Connection` object (or grab it from the pool).
2. Create the `Statement` object.
3. Generate the `ResultSet`.
4. Iterate through the `ResultSet` and process the data, or move the data to a `Collection` structure such as a list, map, or set.
5. Close the `ResultSet`.
6. Close the `Statement`. (Closing the `Statement` will always close the companion `ResultSet`, but you may reuse a `Statement`, so explicitly closing the `ResultSet` is still a good idea.)
7. Close the `Connection` (or release it back to the pool).

As a side note, the reason you can't pass a `ResultSet` is that it depends on the `Statement` and `Connection` used to create it. If the `Statement` is explicitly closed, or closed by garbage collection, while the `ResultSet` is still open, the `ResultSet` will lose its connection to the database. In some cases, this won't matter. However, if the `ResultSet` has cached data, the cache will never be refreshed. Your code won't receive an error message, but you will not be able to access the full set of results.

EXAMPLE

Basic Navigation and Extraction

Sometimes it is appropriate to extract a completely generic set of data from a database and copy it to an in-memory data structure (for caching, passing over a network, etc.). In this example, we copy each row into a `Product` object and place all rows inside a `java.util.List`.

```
public class Product {
  String productName;
  java.util.Date creationDate;
  public Product(String productName, java.util.Date creationDate) {
    this.productName = productName;
    this.creationDate = creationDate;
  }
  public String getProductName() { return productName;}
  public java.util.Date getCreationDate() {return creationDate;}
}
//class wrapper code removed
//try-catch removed
```

```
// Assume statement exists. Copy data into collection.
ResultSet rs = Statement.executeQuery(
    "select product_name, creation_date from products");
java.util.ArrayList list = new java.util.ArrayList();
while ( rs.next() ) {
  String productName = rs.getString(1);
  java.util.Date productDate = rs.getDate(2);
  list.add( new Product(productName, productDate) );
}
```

Listing 3.16 Extracting a ResultSet into a list object

ResultSetMetaData

If you want to make the previous example more generic, you can use a `java.util.Map` and `ResultSetMetaData`. The `Map` will contain name-value pairs for each row. This code is now completely generic and can be used on any `ResultSet`.

```
//Assumes valid statement, try-catch removed
ResultSet rs = statement.executeQuery("select * from products");
ResultSetMetaData metaData = rs.getMetaData();
String[] columnNames = new String[metaData.getColumnCount()];
for (int i = 1; i <= metaData.getColumnCount(); i++) {
  columnNames[i – 1] = metaData.getColumnName(i);
}
java.util.ArrayList list = new java.util.ArrayList();
while ( rs.next() ) {
  java.util.Map rowMap = new java.util.HashMap();
  for (int i = 1; i <= metaData.getColumnCount(); i++) {
    rowMap.put(columnNames[i], rs.getObject(i));  }
  list.add(rowMap);
}
```

Listing 3.17 The generic ResultSet container

HOW AND WHY

How Do I Find Out How Many Rows Were Returned in a SELECT Query?

With a basic `ResultSet`, there is no easy way to determine how many rows were returned. In fact, short of iterating through the `ResultSet` to generate a count, there is no way to find out how many rows were returned.

With a scrollable `ResultSet` (defined in the `Statement` creation), you can take advantage of the `moveLast()`, `getRow()`, and `beforeFirst()` methods. Remember that these methods require a JDBC2.0 or higher driver.

```
/**assumes a valid scrollable ResultSet called rs.  Move to the
last position in the ResultSet, and use getRow(). Rows are
numbered starting at 1, so the number of the last row is the
total number of rows in the ResultSet **/
rs.moveLast();
int numRows = rs.getRow();
//Move back to the beginning to parse results
rs.beforeFirst();
```

Listing 3.18 Counting results

Another alternative is to use a second SELECT query, replacing the requested columns with count(*). This method may be the best alternative, but it requires doubling the number of queries to the database (which adds network traffic, and may not make sense for a small `ResultSet`).

Why Do Some of the ResultSet Navigation Methods Seem Not to Work?

If you are having trouble with the advanced navigation features, you should verify that you are using a driver that supports JDBC 2.0. You should also make sure that you define the `Statement` as scrollable:

```
Statement stmt = conn.createStatement(
ResultSet.TYPE_SCROLL_INSENSITIVE, ResultSet.CONCUR_READ_ONLY);
```

Which getXXXX() Method Should I Use for My Data?

This question has two parts. With regard to choosing between the `getXXXX(int columnIndex)` and `getXXXX(String columnName)` functions, it doesn't really matter. Extracting data by columnName makes code easier to read. However, using columnIndex is less sensitive to database changes.

The second part relates to mapping SQL data types to Java data types. While some mappings are obvious (e.g., `java.lang.String = varchar`), others are more subtle. The following table lists the most common mappings:

SQL Data Type	Java Type	SQL Data Type	Java Type
BIGINT	long	LONGRAW	byte[]
BINARY	byte[]	NUMERIC	java.math.BigDecimal
BIT	bootlean	RAW	byte[]
CHAR	String	REAL	float
DATE	java.sql.Date	SMALLINT	short
DECIMAL	java.math.BigDecimal	TIME	java.sql.Time
DOUBLE	double	TIMESTAMP	java.sql.Timestamp
FLOAT	double	TINYINT	byte
INTEGER	int	VARBINARY	byte[]
LONGVARBINARY	byte[]	VARCHAR	String
LONGVARCHAR	String		

Table 3.2 Generic Java to SQL data-type mappings

Why Can't I Pass a ResultSet Between Class Objects?

The reason it is unsafe to pass a `ResultSet` is that the `ResultSet` depends on the `Statement` and `Connection` objects used to create it. If either of these objects goes out of scope, the `ResultSet` cannot access the database. While this may not seem like a problem, the fact is that most `ResultSet` instances store a limited amount of data in memory, requerying the database for additional rows of data when required. You may find, for instance, that your `ResultSet` will only return the first forty-two rows of a stock portfolio that has over four hundred different stocks! Unfortunately, you cannot override this behavior, because it is directly tied to the way the vendor implements the `Statement` and `ResultSet` interfaces. Generally, if you need to pass the results, you must copy the data from the `ResultSet` into a collection (`List`, `Set`, or `Map`).

What Does "Invalid Cursor State" Mean?

The "Invalid Cursor State" error message is often the result of an attempt to use a `ResultSet` that is not set to a valid row—if, for example, you forgot to use `next()` to move the `ResultSet` to the first row. This error message can also be generated if you use the navigation methods and move out of the range of the `ResultSet`.

BUGS AND CAVEATS

Java and SQL Type Mappings

The `PreparedStatement` and `CallableStatement` objects have `getObject()` and `setObject()` functions that provide generic access to specific database data types. In theory, you should be able to access any data type using `getObject()` or `setObject()`. However, different databases have different mappings between Java and SQL data types. If you want to force a Java type to a specific SQL type, you should provide a hint to the driver. For example:

```
pStatement.setObject(index, myObject, java.sql.Types.INTEGER);
```

Handling Null Values

Quite often databases will contain `null` values. However, Java primitives do not have an equivalent to `null`. Imagine, for example, a case where the database stores an integer value in a column named "months." You would normally use `getInt("months")` to extract the value. Unfortunately, Java has no equivalent to "null" in the integer primitive, so the result is often converted to 0. This could be a big problem if the number 0 has meaning. To avoid the issue, you can use the `wasNull()` method to check for nulls, which can then be converted to a default or safe value.

```
//assumes valid RecordSet called rs
int months = rs.getInt("months");
if (rs.wasNull()) {
  //if months was null, set to -999
  months = -999;
}
```

Listing 3.19 Handling null values

The `wasNull()` function checks the last value extracted from the database, so you must extract the value before checking to see if it was null.

DESIGN NOTES

Data Access Object

JDBC code is relatively easy to use, but it can become messy very quickly. You can spin out JDBC operations into separate "command" objects, known as data access objects, which encapsulate specific database actions into clean Java classes. This idiom is popular when using

Enterprise JavaBeans, which can sometimes have a lot of complex JDBC code CN J2030007.

SUMMARY

`ResultSet` objects allow you to iterate through data returned from an SQL Select statement or stored procedure. Almost every time you use JDBC, you will encounter a `ResultSet`. The important points to remember are:

- A basic `ResultSet` is designed for a single forward pass through the data using `ResultSet.next()`.
- A scrollable `ResultSet` allows advanced iteration, but requires changes to your `Statement.execute()` and `executeQuery()` methods. This feature is part of JDBC 2.0 and may not be implemented by your driver.
- Use the `getXXXX()` methods to extract specific data types from a `ResultSet`. Each method can access a column by name or number.
- `ResultSetMetaData` describes each column in detail.
- A `ResultSet` is always connected to the database by the `Statement` object. Make sure the `Statement` object is open and in scope until you are finished with the `ResultSet`.

Topic: Advanced JDBC

The JDBC 2.0 specification has extended JDBC functionality in many significant ways. This section briefly covers some of the more advanced features, such as transactions, batch processing, `RowSet` objects, and updating a `ResultSet`. Many of these topics include CodeNotes pointers to additional material on the website.

CORE CONCEPTS

Transactions

In most enterprise systems, you will encounter situations where multiple database actions must be performed in an "all or none" manner. A common example is a credit-debit system, where money has to be withdrawn from one account and deposited in another, each account being represented by a row in a table. Unless both updates happen, neither one should. The J2EE specification supports transactions at a much more abstract level with EJBs, which are discussed in Chapter 7 (Enterprise JavaBeans). However, you can perform database-level transactions by using the `Connection.setAutoCommit()` method. The following code fragment illustrates the credit-debit example:

```
/** Code assumes a valid connection called dbConnection.  Wrap
the transaction in its own Try Catch, so you can rollback if
something goes wrong. **/
try {
  //Set autoCommit to false
  dbConnection.setAutoCommit(false);
  //add 100 dollars
  String mySQL = "UPDATE accounts SET balance = balance "
    + "+ 100 WHERE account_id = 'DDCD-1123-CRC1'";
  Statement stmt = dbConnection.createStatement();
  stmt.executeUpdate(mySQL);
  //perform debit of $100
  mySQL = "UPDATE accounts SET balance = balance - 100 where "
    + "account_id = 'ABBA-1421-ABC3'";
  stmt.executeUpdate(mySQL);
  //Commit the statements
  dbConnection.commit();
  //put the connection back into normal mode
  dbConnection.setAutoCommit(true);
}//try
catch (SQLException e) {
  //If something went wrong, we want to rollback the statements
  dbConnection.rollback();
  dbConnection.setAutoCommit(true);
  System.out.println(e.getMessage());
} //catch
```

Listing 3.20 Building a transaction

If you `setAutoCommit()` to false, you must do the following:

1. Always use `commit()` to execute the transaction.
2. Always use `rollback()` in your catch block to revert the changes you may have made.
3. Reset the `Connection` to `setAutoCommit(true)` if you intend to reuse it. If you do not reset the `Connection`, all SQL statements that pass through this `Connection` will be queued until you exe-

cute commit(). If you don't commit(), the statements will never be executed and will be lost when the Connection is closed.

Batch Processing

You can submit multiple statements through a Statement object using batch processing. Batch processing is essentially a limited version of transactions. The difference between the two is that batch processing is limited to a single Statement object, while a transaction can include multiple Statement, CallableStatement, and PreparedStatement objects.

```
/** This fragment needs to be in a try/catch block like the one
used for the transactions example, assumes a valid connection
called dbConnection **/
dbConnection.setAutoCommit(false)
Statement stmt = con.CreateStatement();
String base = "INSERT INTO portfolio VALUES(";
stmt.addBatch(base + " 'SUNW', 19.54)");
stmt.addBatch(base + " 'ORCL', 16.87)");
stmt.addBatch(base + " 'MSFT', 71.38)");
stmt.addBatch(base + " 'IBM', 115.90)");
stmt.executeBatch();
dbConnection.commit();
dbConnection.setAutoCommit(true);
```

Listing 3.21 Batch statements

When you are using batch processing, you may generate multiple SQLExceptions on an execute() statement. You can use SQLException.getNextException() to iterate through all of the errors. For example:

```
catch (SQLException e) {
  System.out.println("SQLException: " + e.getMessage());
  SQLException e2 = e.getNextException();
  while (e2 != null) {
    System.out.println(SQLException: " + e2.getMessage());
    e2 = e.getNextException();
  }
}
```

Listing 3.22 Checking for multiple exceptions

Updating ResultSets

Another new feature introduced in JDBC 2.0 is the ability to update `ResultSets`. A `ResultSet` is updatable if the underlying SQL references a single table and the `ResultSet` is scrollable.

Once you have created an updatable `ResultSet`, you can update the values or insert new ones. Updating a row is a three-step process:

```
//Assumes valid ResultSet called rs
//First step is to navigate to the required row
rs.absolute(13);
/** Second, use the correct updateXXX() method, passing in
either the column name or the column number **/
rs.updateString("PRICE", "80.45");
//Third, execute updateROW() to update the database.
rs.updateRow();
```

Listing 3.23 Updating a ResultSet

Inserting new rows involves a special "staging row" and a four-step process:

```
/** Assumes rs is a valid ResultSet based on a table with three
columns: ticker, qty and price **/
//First, move to staging row
rs.moveToInsertRow();
//Second, add values to row
rs.updateString("ticker", "SUN");
rs.updateInt("qty", 3500);
rs.updateFloat("price", 34.5);
//Third, use the insert statement
rs.insertRow();
//Fourth, move to the new row
rs.moveToCurrentRow();
```

Listing 3.24 Inserting a row into a ResultSet

The RowSet

The `RowSet` object is an extension of the `ResultSet` that is designed to work as a JavaBean. A `RowSet` has two very useful features:

- A `RowSet` can be manipulated by tools designed to work with other JavaBeans. This means you can do anything with a `RowSet` that you would normally do with a JavaBean, including display-

ing it directly to a web page, using it in a GUI, or manipulating it with JavaBean graphical tools.
- Unlike `ResultSets`, certain types of `RowSet` objects can be disconnected from the database. In other words, a disconnected `RowSet` caches the entire contents of the `ResultSet`, does not maintain its `Connection` to the database, and can be easily passed between class objects.

At this time, there are very few complete implementations of `RowSet`. As the specification matures, however, more vendors should start providing support for this object. A `RowSet` example can be found on the website CN J2030004.

DatabaseMetaData

Earlier in the `ResultSet` topic, we discussed using `ResultSetMetaData` to obtain information about a `ResultSet`. The `DatabaseMetaData` object provides the same functionality for discovering information about the database. `DatabaseMetaData` has well over 150 fields and methods that provide information about a database.

In theory, you could use a `DatabaseMetaData` object, along with proper escape clauses, to guarantee true database transparency while retaining access to the advanced features of the various databases. However, the amount of code you would have to write and the amount of time it would take to query the database make this prohibitive.

You can generate a `DatabaseMetaData` object from any `Connection` object using:

```
//Assumes a valid connection called dbConnection
DatabaseMetaData dmd = dbConnection.getMetaData();
```

Some of the more interesting features of `DatabaseMetaData` include:

- `getMaxConnections()`—tells you how many open connections a database will support.
- `getDatabaseProductName()`—returns the name of the database product—for example “ORACLE” or “SQLServer.” Using this method is a good way to determine which SQL syntax you might need to use.
- `getIndexInfo()`, `getTables()`, etc.—return a `ResultSet` with the lists of all indices or tables in the database.

EXAMPLE

Examples for these and other advanced JDBC topics can be found on the CodeNotes website CN J2030005.

HOW AND WHY

When Should I Use Batch Instead of Transactions?

A batch process is limited to a single `Statement`. You should use batch processes only when you need to send a stream of data to the database. Transactions, on the other hand, can be used for multiple statements. Transactions and batch statements are not mutually exclusive. You can use a batch statement inside a transaction.

Why Use a RowSet Instead of a ResultSet?

A `ResultSet` is an open cursor on the database. Good programming practice dictates that a `ResultSet` should be open for as short a time as is possible. A `RowSet`, on the other hand, may be detached from the database and act as a stand-alone data object.

BUGS AND CAVEATS

Using Updatable ResultSets

Whenever you hold a `ResultSet` open, you are holding an open cursor on the database. In other words, you are creating a potential for deadlocks and stale data. Be very careful using updatable `ResultSet` objects in any system that involves multithreading.

Batch Failures

Some databases will continue to execute batch statements after the first error occurs. Other databases will terminate the entire batch at the first error. This behavior is generally determined at the database level. In practice, it makes very little difference, as you will probably want to rollback the entire batch statement.

DESIGN NOTES

When to Use Batch Statements

With a batch statement, you are making fewer trips to the database, but issuing more commands each trip. You should use batch statements when you have many small commands that can be sent as a single package. This will help reduce latency and transactional locks.

SUMMARY

The advanced JDBC features can be very powerful, but require some careful design and planning. Batch processing and transactions force you to think about programming structure, while updatable `ResultSet` and `RowSet` objects require planning for resource contention.

Chapter Summary

JDBC provides a wide range of powerful functions for connecting to a database. You can use the JDBC objects to perform all database access functions common to enterprise systems. As you will see in the following sections, most of the JDBC functionality has been encapsulated into more user-friendly packages, and many vendors have written tools to help manage JDBC code. Most of these tools are designed to work with Enterprise JavaBeans and insulate the developer from having to write redundant SQL statements and JDBC code.

Chapter 4

RMI, JNDI, AND JAVAMAIL

J2EE contains many supporting APIs and technologies that are ancillary to the major components such as Enterprise JavaBeans (Chapter 7). This chapter contains core concepts for three of these APIs: Remote Method Invocation (RMI), Java Naming and Directory Interface (JNDI), and JavaMail.

The intricate details of RMI, JNDI, and JavaMail are beyond the scope of this book. However, the CodeNotes website contains detailed explanations and code examples, as indicated by the pointers below.

Remote Method Invocation (RMI)

Over the years, CORBA (Common Object Request Broker Architecture) and COM (Component Object Model) have come to dominate distributed computing. While Java can integrate with CORBA and COM (via CORBA and COM "bridges"), the J2EE specification also includes an independent remote procedure interface called Remote Method Invocation. RMI is both a simplified architecture and an interchangeable gateway for working with CORBA objects. Both CORBA and RMI can operate over the Internet Inter-ORB Protocol (IIOP) and can therefore talk to each other transparently. RMI is a critical component for building Enterprise JavaBeans, which are fundamentally RMI objects that implement specific interfaces. A short tutorial on RMI can be found on the CodeNotes website CN J2040017.

Java Naming and Directory Interface (JNDI)

JNDI provides a link between Java code and various naming and directory services such as LDAP, Domain Name System (DNS), Novell Directory Service (NDS), CORBA, and Network Information System (NIS). In practice, this means that JNDI allows you to access code and resources across widely separated platforms and directory structures through the use of a simple naming scheme. JNDI can be used for basic naming and directory tasks, including referencing RMI objects through a naming service, as illustrated on the CodeNotes website CN J2040018.

JavaMail

Many enterprise systems need to integrate with e-mail services, particularly when generating notifications of key events. JavaMail can be easily accessed from stand-alone applications, Servlets, JSPs, and Enterprise JavaBeans. JavaMail can be used to send, receive, and manage e-mail, as illustrated on the CodeNotes website CN J2040019

Core Concepts

Distributed Objects

JNDI, JavaMail, and particularly RMI all grew out of the need for distributed computing and distributed objects. Distributed systems began in the late 1970s as Remote Procedure Call (RPC) systems using C, COBOL, or other languages. The advent of object-oriented languages like C++ and Smalltalk brought the need for an object-oriented RPC standard.

In the early 1990s, a vendor consortium of over six hundred companies, the Object Management Group (OMG), defined a specification for object-oriented RPCs and related services, known as the Common Object Request Broker Architecture (CORBA). CORBA allowed several object-oriented (and even non-object-oriented) languages to communicate with each other, over different hardware or operating system platforms, by using a common Interface Definition Language (IDL) and a common network wire protocol, the Internet Inter-ORB Protocol (IIOP).

In the late 1990s, Sun created the Remote Method Invocation API, the standard RPC framework for Java. It was later extended to interoperate with CORBA. This extension was called "RMI/IIOP" and allowed RMI developers to call other CORBA objects from Java or develop Java objects that could be called a CORBA object.

Distributed Information

While the OMG and CORBA were attacking the problem of distributed computing, many companies were working on the problem of distributed information. As applications spread from one machine to many machines, IT departments were faced with the challenge of managing a variety of databases, application servers, network equipment, and information stores. Naming and directory services such as LDAP, Active Directory, Novell Directory Services (NDS), Sun's Network Information Service (NIS), and the Domain Naming Service (DNS) provide a centralized, hierarchical organization structure for wildly disparate data. Naming and directory services map an abstract label to some form of computational resource. The JNDI API provides a simple interface to all naming and directory technologies to access underlying resources from a Java program. Such resources can be physical (such as a printer), data sources (such as a relational databse), business applications (such as EJBs), security information (such as x509 certificates), or shared file systems.

Distributed Communication

E-mail is the true "killer application" of distributed computing. Even though distributed information and computing are important, peer-to-peer communication provides the true value for any computer network. JavaMail provides a common interface to the wide variety of protocols for creating, sending, receiving, and managing e-mail, including the Simple Mail Transport Protocol (SMTP), the Post Office Protocol (POP), Multipurpose Internet Mail Extensions (MIME), and the Internet Message Access Protocol (IMAP).

Chapter Summary

JNDI and RMI are both systems for distributed computing. JNDI provides access to data that is available through a variety of naming services or is hidden in a directory service. RMI, on the other hand, is a method for a remote client to access a server object as if it existed as part of the client. JavaMail provides methods of sending and receiving e-mail, which may be the most important distributed computing system of all. All three of these APIs will appear again in the following topics.

Chapter 5

SERVLETS

It can be argued that in the early days of the Web, the Internet was basically a glorified file-transfer system. A client would request a file from a server and the server would deliver the file to the client. Basic file-transfer protocols (e.g., ftp and gopher) gave way to formatted content (HTML) and the Hyper Text Tranfer Protcol (HTTP). The client still requested a file, and the server still delivered it, but then the client's browser automatically rendered and displayed the file.

The next evolutionary step was the design of interactive web pages and dynamic content. The server became more complicated and versatile. Paradigms like CGI (Common Gateway Interface) and Microsoft's ASP gave servers the ability to dynamically generate HTML files in response to user input. The client browser also became more sophisticated, accepting and running small programs (applets and ActiveX controls). However, most server-side programming was limited to single-threaded, resource-intensive executables (e.g., CGI systems), or to specific vendors and hardware platforms (e.g., Netscape's Livewire server-side scripting). Client-side programming suffered from slow download times, insecure environments, and incompatible interfaces.

Sun introduced Java Servlets as a means of leveraging the multiplatform nature of Java for server-side programming. Servlets are compiled Java classes that are executed and maintained by a Servlet container. Unlike traditional CGI programs, a Servlet can have a life cycle greater than an individual page. In other words, Servlets can share resources.

Servlets are also designed to take advantage of state, or the ability to maintain user data over extended periods of time.

This chapter illustrates the basic concepts of Servlets and introduces many of the topics that will be further explored in Chapter 6 (JavaServer Pages).

Simple Application

Servlet technology allows you to develop Java applications that generate web content. The HelloServlet example illustrates some of the basic properties of a Servlet. The example has two sections: the code and the configuration.

```
import java.io.*;
import javax.servlet.*;
import javax.servlet.http.*;
public class HelloServlet extends HttpServlet {
  public void doGet(HttpServletRequest request,
      HttpServletResponse response)
      throws IOException, ServletException {
    String text = request.getParameter("subject");
    if (text == null) {text = "World";}
      //Write page
      response.setContentType("text/html");
      PrintWriter out = response.getWriter();
      out.println("<html>");
      out.println("<body>");
      out.println("<h1>Hello " + text + "</h1>");
      out.println("</body>");
      out.println("</html>");
    }
}
```

Listing 5.1a   HelloServlet

Once you have built and compiled the Servlet, you should add the following XML to the web.xml deployment descriptor in your application WEB-INF directory (e.g., C:\webdev\WEB-INF\web.xml). Remember that this descriptor was built in the “Creating a Web Application” section of Chapter 2 (Installation).

```
<servlet>
  <servlet-name>HelloServlet</servlet-name>
  <servlet-class>HelloServlet</servlet-class>
</servlet>
<servlet-mapping>
  <servlet-name>HelloServlet</servlet-name>
  <url-pattern>/HelloServlet</url-pattern>
</servlet-mapping>
```

Listing 5.1b The descriptor for HelloServlet

If you access the page with the basic URL (e.g., http://localhost:8080/CodeNotes/HelloServlet), the output will be

```
Hello World
```

However, if you access the page with a URL that has a "subject" parameter in the HTTP query string (e.g., CodeNotes/HelloServlet?subject=CodeNotes%20Reader), the output will be

```
Hello CodeNotes Reader
```

Core Concepts

Prerequisites

As a quick refresher, you should have already done the following:

1. Created a web application directory called C:\webdev. When you create a Servlet, you should put it in the "WEB-INF\classes" subdirectory (e.g., C:\webdev\WEB-INF\classes).
2. Installed and started Tomcat. To start Tomcat on Windows, you need to open a command window and launch the startup.bat file (e.g., C:\Jakarta\bin\startup.bat). If you are using a different Servlet container, make sure it is properly installed, configured, and running.

If you haven't built an application directory, or do not know how to install or start the Tomcat server, please refer to the Web Applications topic in Chapter 2 (Installation).

Key Vocabulary

Servlets and JavaServer Pages (JSPs) share many of the same core concepts and vocabulary. These terms apply equally to both JSPs and Servlets:

- Buffer—The buffer is the holding tank between the server and the client. Using JSP or Servlets, you can control the buffer's size, content, and actions.
- Servlet—A Servlet is a compiled Java class that is managed by a Servlet Container and exposes "web-page-like" functionality. A Servlet is conceptually similar to a CGI executable except that it is managed by a container (e.g., Tomcat) and can maintain state between client requests.
- JavaServer Page (JSP)—JavaServer Pages are "HTML-like" documents that contain Java code. A JSP container compiles a JSP into a Servlet the first time the page is requested.
- Container—Both Servlets and JSPs rely on a container. The container performs many housekeeping functions (such as exposing common objects), maintains the life cycle of the Servlet or JSP, and either interfaces with or is part of the web server.
- Cookie—A cookie is a small text file that is stored on the client. A cookie contains arbitrary name-value pairs and is often used to store user preferences and other client-specific information. HTTP is a fundamentally stateless protocol, so cookies are often used to keep track of client state between page requests.
- Engine—This term persists from the original specification for Servlets but has been supplanted by the concept of a container (see above).
- Web server—The web server is a stand-alone application that handles the housekeeping chores of accepting, translating, and broadcasting content over HTTP.

Servlet Page Life Cycle

When a user (client browser) requests a page that is a Servlet, the request is first processed by the web server. The web server redirects the request to the Servlet container. The container will create an instance of the appropriate Servlet (if one doesn't already exist) and pass a request and a response object into the Servlet's `service()` method. The Servlet will then execute either the `doGet()` or `doPost()` method and create the HTML output. The container passes the output back to the web server through the response object, then on to the client browser.

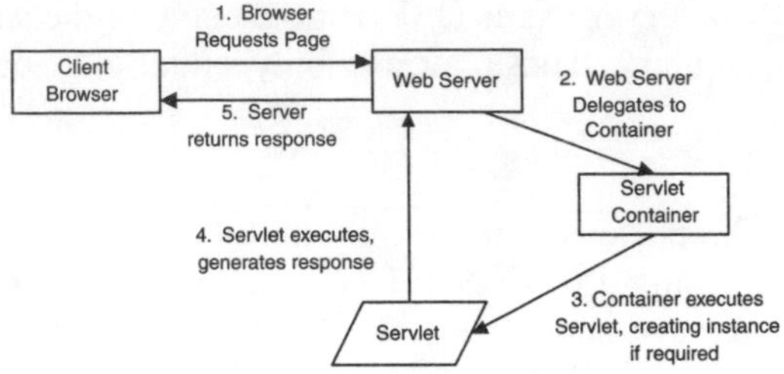

Figure 5.1 The basic Servlet life cycle

This basic life cycle can be modified in many ways. A Servlet can connect to another Servlet, a web page, or a JSP. A Servlet can also instantiate other Java classes and perform actions such as connecting to a database or sending an e-mail.

Servlet Configuration

Every time you create a new Servlet, you must reconfigure the web application by modifying the deployment descriptor. Fortunately, the configuration step is minor. Unfortunately, some Servlet containers require that you stop and restart the server in order to add a new Servlet.

If you are using Tomcat, and you set up the application as directed in Chapter 2 (Installation), then your application context should have a parameter called "reloadable," which should be set to "true." This parameter tells Tomcat to check for "unregistered" Servlets when it receives a request for an unfamiliar page.

In order to register a Servlet with your application, you must add a couple of new XML nodes to the application's web.xml descriptor file (e.g., c:\webdev\WEB-INF\web.xml). These basic nodes should be placed inside the <web-app> tags, and should look like:

```
<servlet>
  <servlet-name>name</servlet-name>
  <servlet-class>ClassName</servlet-class>
</servlet>
<servlet-mapping>
  <servlet-name>name</servlet-name>
  <url-pattern>ServletURL</url-pattern>
</servlet-mapping>
```

Listing 5.2 Adding a Servlet to the application

The name is arbitrary and is used as a link between the Servlet class and the Servlet URL. The Servlet class is the name (and possibly package) for the Servlet (e.g., HelloServlet), whereas the URL pattern is the relative URL for the Servlet (e.g., /HelloServlet). Note that if several Servlets are listed in the file, all of the <servlet> nodes must be grouped together. Similarly, all <servlet-mapping> tags must be grouped together after the <servlet> tags.

The various details of deployment descriptors are described in Chapter 8 (Packaging and Deployment).

State, Scope, and Context

The terms "state," "scope," and "context" are often used interchangeably in reference to web pages. However, each term has a specific meaning and a specific use.

State

State refers to the ability to save information. An application that "remembers" data from one page to the next is said to "maintain state" or to be "stateful." A basic HTML page does not retain information between HTTP requests and is thus "stateless." Maintaining state is a particularly important concept for useful web applications such as e-commerce systems.

State can be maintained in any number of ways, from client-side cookies to database tables. State can also last for any length of time, from a single page access to a single user session to permanent storage.

Scope

Scope is often described as the lifespan of state, or the length of time over which state is maintained and can be accessed. Servlets and JSP have four basic levels of scope:

- Page—The page scope is defined as the time between the initialization of a particular page and its destruction. Data stored in the page scope retains state as long as the page remains active. Page scope is only available for JSPs.
- Session—The session scope consists of a single interactive conversation between a client and a web server. Data stored in the session scope maintains state until the session is destroyed through timeout, or through closing the browser(s) that accessed the site, or through a communications failure. The session scope is a very common place to store information that relates to a particular user (such as authentication) or a particular web experience (such as a shopping cart).
- Application—The application scope relates to all of the Servlets and JSPs that are part of a Java web application. This scope tran-

scends individual users and is often used for hit counters and support systems (e.g., JDBC connection pools). Application scope is maintained until the server is restarted or the application is redeployed.

- Request—The request scope relates specifically to the request that launched the page. A request scope can be forwarded through several Servlets and JSPs and maintains its state until a response object is sent in reply to the client.

Topic: Basic Servlets

Servlets are simply Java classes that follow three basic rules:

- An HTTP Servlet must extend `javax.servlet.http.HttpServlet` (or extend an abstract class that does).
- The Servlet must implement at least one of the following methods: `doGet()`, `doPost()`, `doPut()`, `doDelete()`, `init()`, `destroy()`, or `service()`.
- The servlet can optionally implement `init()`, `destroy()`, or `getServletInfo()`.

However, there is much more to Servlets than the implementation of a few simple methods. This topic begins with the basic methods and then provides some examples of the suprising power of basic Servlets.

CORE CONCEPTS

HTTP Methods and service()

All HTTP network requests have several "methods" of invocation that indicate the intent of the request, such as `GET`, `POST`, `PUT`, and `DELETE`. In practice, only `GET` and `POST` methods are used. When a Servlet container first routes to a Servlet, it invokes the `service()` method. By default, the `service()` method will dispatch to `doGet()`, `doPost()`, `doPut()`, or `doDelete()` based on the method information given in the HTTP request header. You can override this default `service()` implementation to respond to all HTTP requests in an identical way, although you would usually just override `doGet()` or `doPost()`.

Get

The GET method is the most common form of HTTP request. The `doGet()` method receives an `HttpServletRequest` and an `HttpServletResponse` object (both described in the next topic, on support objects) and must throw `java.io.IOException` and `ServletException`.

A simple implementation might look like this:

```
public void doGet (HttpServletRequest req, HttpServletResponse res)
    throws ServletException, IOException {
  res.setContentType("text/html");
  PrintWriter out = res.getWriter();
  out.println("Hello World");
}
```

Listing 5.3   The basic DoGet method

Post

HTTP employs the POST method to transfer large amounts of HTML form data. The `doPost()` method is called much like `doGet()`. If the Servlet's `service()` method receives an HTTP POST request, the Servlet's `doPost()` method is called. The input parameters are identical to `doGet()`. The `doPost()` method is sometimes chained to `doGet()`:

```
public void doPost (HttpServletRequest req,
    HttpServletResponse res) throws ServletException, IOException {
  doGet(req, res);
}
```

Listing 5.4   Chaining DoPost to DoGet

Init and Destroy

The init and destroy methods identify the beginning and end of the Servlet life cycle. The `init()` method is called when a Servlet is being placed into service by the container, and the `destroy()` method is called when the container takes the Servlet out of service. These methods are most often used to initalize and release resources, or to provide other life cycle–sensitive support functions.

ServletInfo

The `getServletInfo()` method can be overridden to provide information such as the Servlet author, company, copyright, or version. This method returns an empty string by default and is normally only called by other Servlets.

EXAMPLE

This is an example of a very basic Servlet:

```
package com.codenotes.j2ee.servlet;
import javax.servlet.*;
import javax.servlet.http.*;
import java.io.*;
public class ExampleServlet extends HttpServlet {
  public void doGet(HttpServletRequest request,
      HttpServletResponse response)
      throws ServletException, IOException {
    response.setContentType("text/html");
    PrintWriter out = response.getWriter();
    out.println("<HTML>");
    out.println("  <BODY>");
    out.println("  <P>Hello, Servlet World!</P>");
    out.println("  </BODY>");
    out.println("</HTML>");
  }
}
```

Listing 5.5 A simple Servlet

This next example is a little more complicated and parses the content of an HTML form. Assume we have a basic HTML form with two text fields and a SUBMIT button. In HTML:

```
<HTML>
<BODY>
  An adding calculator.
  <FORM METHOD="POST" ACTION="CalculatorServlet">
    <P>X Value: <INPUT NAME="xValue" TYPE="TEXT"></P>
    <P>Y Value: <INPUT NAME="yValue" TYPE="TEXT"></P>
    <INPUT TYPE="SUBMIT">
  </FORM>
</BODY>
</HTML>
```

Listing 5.6a The basic form

We can write a Servlet (CalculatorServlet) that will take the two numbers submitted in the previous form, add them, and write the result to an HTML page. The Servlet code might look like this:

```
public class CalculatorServlet extends HttpServlet {
  public void doPost(HttpServletRequest request,
      HttpServletResponse response)
      throws ServletException, IOException {
    //Extract the values
    int xValue = Integer.parseInt((String)
      request.getParameter("xValue"));
    int yValue = Integer.parseInt((String)
      request.getParameter("yValue") );
    int result = xValue + yValue;
    //Write the output
    response.setContentType("text/html");
    PrintWriter out = response.getWriter();
    out.println("<HTML>");
    out.println("  <BODY>");
    out.println("  <P>The result is:</P>");
    out.println("  <P>" + xValue + " + " + yValue + " = "
       + result + "</P>");
    out.println("  </BODY>");
    out.println("</HTML>");
  }
}
```

Listing 5.6b The CalcluatorServlet

HOW AND WHY

When Do I Use the destroy() Method?

The `destroy()` method is called whenever the server shuts down or the container terminates the Servlet. Generally this method is used to release any system resources such as a `javax.sql.Datasource`.

BUGS AND CAVEATS

All attempts to point a web browser to a Servlet will result in an HTTP `GET` request by default. The only way to perform an HTTP `POST` request is to submit a form using the `METHOD="POST"` attribute in the `<FORM>` HTML tag, as show in Listing 5.6a.

Also note that if you attempt to browse to a Servlet that only implements `doPost()`, you will receive an HTTP 405 error, indicating that the URL does not support the `GET` method. Overriding the `doGet()` method would enable the Servlet to handle such requests.

DESIGN NOTES

An HTML Helper Class

As you can see from the examples, quite a bit of Servlet code contains standard HTML patterns such as <TITLE>This is my Title</TITLE>. When you are developing several Servlets, writing this standard code becomes tedious and distracts you from building your specific functionality. To combat this, you could build a set of standard HTML helper functions for common tasks such as:

- Building the header (pass in the title string, return header string), including cascading style sheets (CSS):

```
<HTML>
<LINK rel="stylesheet" type="text/css" href="base.css" />
<HEADER><TITLE>titlestring</TITLE></HEADER>
```

- Building standard table rows (pass in a `String` array with the values, return a `String` that is a formatted table row).

Extending HttpServlet

In some cases, you may want to subclass `HttpServlet` and add helper functions and variables that will be common to all of your Servlets. For example, if you have a set of Servlets that requires database access, you may want to create a `JdbcHttpServlet` class that establishes the database connection pool. Your database Servlets could extend `JdbcHttpServlet` and automatically inherit the code. This pattern is illustrated on the CodeNotes website CN `J2050001`.

SUMMARY

A basic Servlet is simply a Java class that extends `javax.Servlet.http.HttpServlet` and implements at least one of the Servlet methods, typically `doGet()` or `doPost()`.

Once you have compiled the Servlet, don't forget to register it in the web.xml file.

Topic: Support Objects

The Servlet container does more than just create and destroy Servlet instances. It also provides instances of several support objects such as `HttpServletRequest` and `HttpServletResponse`. These support objects are very useful for building complex web applications. Each of the commonly used objects is detailed in the following sections.

The support objects will appear again in the Implicit Objects topic in Chapter 6 (JavaServer Pages).

CORE CONCEPTS

The PrintWriter (java.io.PrintWriter)

One of the first steps in using a Servlet is setting up the `java.io.PrintWriter`. The `PrintWriter` is a text pipeline into the `HttpServletResponse` object, which sends the HTML output to the client. In order to set the `PrintWriter`, you generally set the MIME content type for the page, and then instantiate the writer.

```
response.setContentType("text/html");
java.io.PrintWriter out = res.getWriter();
```

Listing 5.7 Creating the PrintWriter

Anything that you write to the `PrintWriter` will be sent to the client browser.

Attributes

Several of the helper objects (`HttpServletRequest`, `HttpServletContext`, `HttpSession`) share the ability to store and retrieve attributes that make up the state of the Servlet. Each object holds attributes in a particular scope (request, application, and session level, respectively). An attribute is simply a key-value pair where the key is a `String` and the value is a `java.lang.Object`. The methods for accessing attributes are common to all four objects:

Method	Description
getAttribute(key)	Returns the value associated with the key
getAttributeNames()	Returns a String array of all the current attribute names
setAttribute(key, value)	Adds a new attribute, or updates an existing attribute with a new value
removeAttribute(key)	Removes the attribute

Table 5.1 Methods for accessing implicit object attributes

The key is a `java.lang.String` object and is case-sensitive. There are no restrictions on the content of the key; however, you should avoid using obscure strings and special characters, as they are hard to read.

The attribute value is stored as a generic `java.lang.Object`. You can store any type of object as an attribute. However, you must be careful to cast the object to the proper type when you want to use it. Also, you must encapsulate the primitives (`int`, `float`, `double`, `byte`, `short`, `long`, etc.) using the wrapper classes (`Int`, `Float`, `Double`, `Byte`, `Short`, `Long`). The following example illustrates this type of casting:

```
request.setAttribute("number", new Float(42.5));
// No conversion if we write to buffer, toString() is implied
out.print("Is this 42.5? ");
out.println(request.getAttribute("number"));
/** if you want to do math or access the number, then cast back
to a float **/
out.print("Some math:  42.5 + 30.3 = ");
Float number = (Float)request.getAttribute("number"))
out.println(number.floatValue() + 30.3f);
```

Listing 5.8 Casting Attributes

HttpServletRequest

The request object provides access to the initial request that has launched the page. You can use this object to retrieve any request parameters, HTTP headers, cookies, request scope attributes, and other information related to the request issued by the browser. The major methods for this object can be divided into three groups: query strings, HTTP headers, and miscellaneous methods.

Query String

An HTML form organizes data into a query sting that is sent to the URL specified in the <FORM> tag's `ACTION` attribute. On HTTP `GET` methods, the query string is appended to the URL using a question mark ("?") to denote where the request string begins. On `POST` invocations, the request string is not appended to the URL but sent transparently along with the network request. A query string is composed of key-value pairs separated by the "&" symbol. The parameter key and its value(s) are exposed as `java.lang.String` objects, which may need conversion to the appropriate types for your application.

A typical request string might be:

```
/CodeNotes/GetBookList?series=CodeNotes&book=J2EE&book=XML
```

The HttpRequest object provides methods for extracting any or all parts of this string. In all cases, the name parameter is case-sensitive.

- `getParameter(name)`—Returns the value of the first instance of the named parameter. Returns `null` if the parameter is not found.
- `getParameterNames()`—Returns a `java.util.Enumeration` with the names of all parameters in the query string
- `getParameterValues(name)`—Returns a string array of all of the values for a named parameter
- `getMethod()`—Returns the HTTP method, which is either `Get` or `Post`
- `getRequestURI()`—Returns a string containing a URI path up to the QueryString. (Note that the method ends with URI, not URL!)
- `getQueryString()`—Returns the full query string

Note that the `getParameterNames()` method returns a `java.util.Enumeration` object. If you want to display the values in this object, you will need to import `java.util.Enumeration` (or `java.util.*`) and iterate through the object using code like this:

```
java.util.Enumeration params = request.getParameterNames();
while (params.hasMoreElements()) {
  out.print(params.nextElement() + "<BR>");
}
```

Listing 5.9 Accessing parameter names

Similarly, the `getParameterValues()` object returns a `String` array. The quickest way to print the entire contents of a `String` array is to use the helper methods in the `Arrays` class:

```
String values[] = request.getParameterValues("book");
out.println("getParameterValues:" + Arrays.asList(values));
```

Listing 5.10 Accessing parameter values

HTTP Headers

The next set of `HttpServletRequest` methods returns HTTP header information. HTTP request headers are generated by the user's browser and contain metainformation about the request. For example, you can extract the "User-Agent" header to find information about the browser. Unlike parameter values, the name argument for HTTP headers is *not* case-sensitive.

HttpServletResponse

The `HttpServletResponse` object is the counterpart object to `HttpServletRequest`. Whereas the request tells you everything about the initiation of the page, response allows you to control the output of the page. The response object methods deal with the creation of HTTP headers, content specification, and the handling of URLs for redirecting a page. Most important, the response object is the conduit for sending data back to the client browser. You can find more information about content type and character sets on the CodeNotes website CN J2050002.

HTTP Header Methods

The response header methods are the counterparts to the HTTP methods in the `HttpServletRequest` object. You can use these methods to create HTTP headers that will be sent to the client in the response.

One of the more practical uses of these methods is to prevent a web page from being cached by a browser. Because different browsers support HTTP headers in different fashions, this fragment uses three methods to try to stop the browser from caching the page.

```
/** This code acts on the HttpServletResponse object named res
and a HttpServletRequest object named req.  First, set the
expires header into the past.  Most browsers will not re-use
expired pages.**/
res.setDateHeader("Expires", 0);
/** Next, set a "Pragma" header that tells HTTP 1.0 browsers not
```

```
to cache the page **/
res.setHeader("Pragma", "no-cache");
/** Finally, use the HTTP 1.1 "Cache-Control" header to
explicitly tell HTTP 1.1 browsers not to cache the page **/
if (req.getProtocol().equals("HTTP/1.1")) {
  res.setHeader("Cache-Control", "no-cache");
}
```

Listing 5.11 Preventing the browser from caching a page

Navigation Methods

The HttpResponse object has three important navigation methods.

- sendRedirect()—This method sends a new URL to the client and forces the client to the new page. The sendRedirect() method will destroy the current buffer before redirecting the client. In other words, if you build half of your page, then use the sendRedirect() method, the client will not see any content from the original Servlet.
- encodeRedirectURL()—Before you can use the sendRedirect() method, you should use this function to add the session id. This method will add the session id only if the page is required to maintain state. The decision to add the id is purely up to the container.
- encodeURL()—In every case except for the sendRedirect() method, you should use encodeURL() to prepare the page reference. This method will add the session id if it is required. Because the decision on whether state is required is different for sendRedirect() than for other flow control methods (such as an HTML form), the encodeURL() method uses different logic than encodeRedirectURL().

Both encodeURL() and encodeRedirectURL() accept path names that are relative to the web application context. For example, the following code would create a form that sends the user to the Checkout Servlet, which is in the "servlets" folder:

```
//fragment.  In doGet or doPost with printWriter set.
out.println("<form action="
  + response.encodeURL("/Servlet/Checkout") + " method=post >");
```

Listing 5.12 Using encodeURL()

javax.servlet.http.HttpSession

The session object provides a "stateful" context across multiple page requests from the same client during a conversation with the server. In other words, once a user has connected to the website, the session object will be available to all of the Servlets and JSPs that the user accesses until the session is closed due to timeout or error. You can access the `HttpSession` object for a Servlet using the following code:

```
//Inside doGet() or doPost()
HttpSession session = req.getSession();
```

Listing 5.13 Accessing the HttpSession

If the session does not exist, this method will automatically create one. Otherwise, you will be able to access the existing session.

Attributes

The most commonly used feature of the session object is the attribute storage. Remember that attributes are attached to several support objects and are the means for storing web state in a particular scope. Session attributes are commonly used to store user values (such as name and authentication) and other information that needs to be shared between pages. For example, you could easily store an e-commerce shopping cart JavaBean in a session attribute. When the user selects the first product, a new shopping cart bean would be created and stored in the session object. Any shopping page would have access to the cart, regardless of how the user navigates between pages. The code on the shopping page might look like this:

```
//Create new attribute if shopping cart does not exist
//Assumes ShoppingCartBean object has been imported
HttpSession session = req.getSession();
if (session.getAttribute("Cart") == null) {
  ShoppingCartBean cart = new ShoppingCartBean();
} else {
  ShoppingCartBean cart =
    (ShoppingBeanCart)session.getAttribute("Cart");
}
/**Next, add new product to cart.  Assumes ItemBean is a valid
object and has been imported **/
ItemBean newItem = new ItemBean("Hat", 1, 23.34, "UPC343212");
cart.addItem(newItem);
/**Then, add or update the session attribute Remember that
```

```
attribute names ARE case-sensitive. **/
session.setAttribute("Cart", cart);
```

Listing 5.14 Using attributes

Session Management

Generally, you can leave session management to the container. When you need to manage a session programmatically, you can adjust the timeout interval and manually discard a session. The following methods are part of the `HttpSession` object:

- `MaxInactiveInterval()`—The session object has get and set methods for controlling the maximum time (in seconds) between user requests. If a user does not perform a request in that time, the session object is destroyed. The default setting is container-specific, but is generally 1,800 seconds (30 minutes).
- `invalidate()`—The `invalidate()` method will destroy the session object and release references to objects stored in the session attributes.
- `getId()`—Session IDs provide a temporary primary key that you can use to identify a session uniquely. The session id is generated by the JSP container and may use any system the vendor chooses. For example, Tomcat generates a ten-character alphanumeric id such as "1juorqf451". ids may be reused, although active sessions will never share ids. The id is usually sent to the client as a cookie or part of the query string to help the container maintain the session link to a particular `HttpSession` object.
- `getCreationTime()` and `getLastAccessedTime()`—These methods will return date objects that tell you when the session was created and when it was last accessed.

javax.servlet.ServletContext

The `ServletContext` object is very similar to the `HttpSession` object, except that the scope is wider. The `ServletContext` provides application-level scope, which includes all of the pages that are incorporated into the application directory or Web Archive (WAR) file. Remember that when you set up Tomcat, you created an application called "webdev." All of the pages in "webdev" share a common `ServletContext`. The Tomcat sample pages (in an application called "sample") share a different `ServletContext` instance.

The most commonly used application methods relate to attributes, information and utility functions, and logging. Application attributes differ from session attributes only in terms of their scope. Unlike session attributes, application attributes are not tied to a particular user. Instead, thse attributes are global to a single web application on a single JVM.

Information and Utility Functions

The `ServletContext` object can be used to extract information about the container and the web server. This information may be useful in establishing web applications that are deployable across multiple containers. These functions are illustrated on the CodeNotes website CN J2050003.

Logging

The `ServletContext` object also provides access to the log files for the application. You can use the `log()` method to write a new message to the output log:

```
//inside doPost() or doGet()
HttpServletContext application = req.getServletConfig();
application.log("Wrote a message with the log function.");
```

Listing 5.15a The log function

Within an `HttpServlet` object, you can access the log directly through a built-in convenience function, which encapsulates this:

```
//The Log method is built into the Servlet class
Log("Wrote a log message with less typing");
```

Listing 5.15b An alternate log function

As mentioned in the setup section, the location and storage of the log files are container-specific. Some containers actually use several different log files. Tomcat, for example, uses a log file for Servlet messages (logs/Servlet.log), a second file for page requests (logs/jasper.log), and a third file for container and error messages. By default, the third file is written directly to the console or command window.

java.servlet.RequestDispatcher

In addition to the `sendRedirect()` methods mentioned with the `HttpServletResponse` object, the `RequestDispatcher` object provides two more methods for controlling application flow. The `forward()` and `include()` methods provide access to web resources without sending data to the client. In other words, you can use the `RequestDispatcher` to create chained Servlets or Servlet filters.

The forward() Method

`RequestDispatcher.forward()` is used to transfer control *permanently* to another Servlet (or JSP). The `forward()` method is a server-side control transfer. The client browser will never know that a new Servlet has been accessed. The new Servlet will receive the current `HttpServletRequest` and `HttpServletResponse` objects and the associated session information. Unfortunately, you can't use this method if you have already used a `PrintWriter` to send data to the client. An `IllegalStateException` will be thrown.

Don't forget that this method exists in part of an active function in the calling Servlet. If you do not explicitly commit the output in the second Servlet (closing the output buffer), the container will return to the calling Servlet and continue execution. There are two ways of working around this, illustrated in following code fragments:

```
//In Servlet 1 (Main Servlet)
public doGet(...){
  if (loginOK ) {
    getServletContext().getRequestDispatcher(
      "servlet/Servlet2").forward(request,response);
    //Choice 1, explicitly exit the subroutine.
    return;
  }
  out.println("<H1>Login Unsuccessful</H1>");
  }
}


/**Choice 2, inside Servlet2.  This will cause the container to
ignore any following out.println commands **/
public doGet(...)
  ...
  // close and implicitly flush the output to the client
  out.close();
```

Listing 5.16 Working with forward()

The include() Method

`RequestDispatcher.include()` is similar to `forward()` except that it *temporarily* transfers control to another Servlet. When the second Servlet is finished, control is returned to the original Servlet. This method is particularly useful for accessing "helper Servlets" that perform specific tasks or generate standard HTML content such as banners, tabled results, etc.

Exceptions

The container generally handles Servlet exceptions by redirecting the browser to a standard error page defined in the web application deployment descriptor (see Chapter 8). The Servlet specification also includes two new Exceptions.

The first (`javax.servlet.ServletException`) is a generic exception that can be thrown under any circumstance. The second (`javax.servlet.UnavailableException`) should be thrown when a Servlet is unable to handle requests. These exceptions are commonly thrown either when configuration information has been corrupted or network access to critical resources (e.g., a database) has been lost.

EXAMPLE

The following (admittedly trivial) example illustrates the `HttpRequest` object and the `RequestDispatcher`. The first Servlet (GetTheDate.java) will forward to the second Servlet (ShowTheDate.java).

```
import javax.servlet.*;
import javax.servlet.http.*;
import java.io.*;
import java.text.*;
import java.util.*;
public class GetTheDate extends HttpServlet {
  public void doGet(HttpServletRequest request,
      HttpServletResponse response)
      throws ServletException, IOException {
    String todaysDate =
      DateFormat.getDateInstance().format(new Date());
    request.setAttribute("todaysDate", todaysDate);
    RequestDispatcher dispatcher =
      getServletContext().getRequestDispatcher("/ShowTodaysDate");
    dispatcher.forward(request, response);
```

```
      return;
    }
}
```

Listing 5.17a The GetTheDate Servlet

```
import javax.servlet.*;
import javax.servlet.http.*;
import java.io.*;
import java.text.*;
import java.util.*;
public class ShowTheDate extends HttpServlet {
  public void doGet(HttpServletRequest request,
       HttpServletResponse response)
       throws ServletException, IOException {
    String todaysDate = (String)request.getAttribute("todaysDate");
    response.setContentType("text/html");
    PrintWriter out = response.getWriter();
    out.println("<HTML>");
    out.println("  <BODY>");
    out.println("  <P>Today's date is: " + todaysDate + "</P>");
    out.println("  </BODY>");
    out.println("</HTML>");
  }
}
```

Listing 5.17b The ShowTheDate Servlet

Finally, the following descriptor should be added to your web.xml file inside the <web-app> tags:

```
<servlet>
  <servlet-name>GetTheDate</servlet-name>
  <servlet-class>
    com.codenotes.j2ee.servlet.GetTheDate
  </servlet-class>
</servlet>
<servlet>
  <servlet-name>ShowTheDate</servlet-name>
  <servlet-class>
    com.codenotes.j2ee.servlet.ShowTheDate
  </servlet-class>
</servlet>
```

```
<servlet-mapping>
  <servlet-name>GetTheDate</servlet-name>
  <url-pattern>GetTodaysDate</url-pattern>
</servlet-mapping>
<servlet-mapping>
  <servlet-name>ShowTheDate</servlet-name>
  <url-pattern>ShowTodaysDate</url-pattern>
</servlet-mapping>
```

Listing 5.17c The descriptor for the date example

Assuming you are using the "CodeNotes" web application defined in Chapter 1, you would call the first Servlet using:

```
http://YourComputer:8080/CodeNotes/GetTodaysDate
```

and you would never know that the container has forwarded you to the `ShowTheDate` Servlet.

HOW AND WHY

Where Should I Store My Crosspage Data (Request, Session, or Application)?

The answer depends on how long you will need the data and which pages will need access to it. The best policy is to use the smallest possible scope. For example, when data has to be shared between two pages that are directly linked through a `RequestDispatcher` action, use the `HttpServletRequest` object. When data has to be shared over several pages but is user-specific, use the `HttpSession` object. When data has to be shared over all the pages in an application regardless of the user session, then use the `HttpServletContext` object.

What Is the Difference Between Writing to log() and System.out()?

In most containers, `System.out` is redirected to a log file and writes output immediately. The `log()` method, on the other hand, is generally buffered and dumped to the log as necessary. In the case of Tomcat, `System.out` is redirected (by default) to the console or command window where the container is running. If you do not change the Tomcat setting to write to a log file, the `System.out` messages may be lost. Although you can use `System.out` to print status messages, using `log()` is more predictable in terms of where the output will go, and it may be faster.

What Is the Difference Between HttpResponse.sendRedirect() and RequestDispatcher.forward()?

The `sendRedirect()` method leverages HTTP's built-in redirect feature to send a message back to the client and force the client to request a new page. The `forward()` method transfers the `HttpServletRequest` and `HttpServletResponse` methods to the indicated file on the server. The `forward()` method never communicates with the client. Use `sendRedirect()` if you do not need the `HttpServletRequest` or `HttpServletResponse` objects, or if you are forwarding to a different application or server. Use `forward()` to build a chain of Servlets inside your application.

BUGS AND CAVEATS

Multithreading

Servlets are run in a multithreaded environment, where many instances of the same Servlet might exist on the same Java Virtual Machine. Use extreme care with (or avoid) instance variables and static variables, because this data is shared between Servlet instances.

The Servlet API includes a marker interface, `SingleThreadModel`, that enables Servlets to assume thread safety. This comes at the expense of reduced performance, since the Servlet container must now create a new Servlet instance for each concurrent HTTP request.

Application Scope

Some Servlet containers can run in a clustered environment, where several JVMs on several machines can service HTTP requests for a single web application. The problem with this setup is that a `ServletContext` object exists for each JVM in a cluster and does not share its attributes between JVMs. In such a situation, you should not rely on application scope to store anything but constant data, since updates to attributes will not be consistent between JVMs.

DESIGN NOTES

Application Flow

Use the `RequestDispatcher` methods to handle your application flow. The `Forward()` and `Include()` methods can be used to tie several Servlets together into a single composite page. For example, you can use the `Include()` method to generate preformatted headers and footers for your page. A Servlet could also be used to handle database operations and then `forward()` on to the next Servlet or JSP responsible for presenting the next screen.

SUMMARY

Without these support objects, it is almost impossible to write a useful web application. Take advantage of the support objects to store data, control application flow, and prepare user output.

Topic: Cookies

A cookie is a small text file that is stored on the client system. The file contains a single name-value pair and several configuration parameters. If you can find the cookie directory on your local machine, you should see many small (1 kb) text files with names such as *yourname*@codenotes[1].txt. If you open this file, you might see a few lines of text that look like:

```
CP
null*
espn.go.com/
0
1761935360
30785590
3250662352
29417438
*
```

Listing 5.18 The content of a cookie

The first line is the cookie name. The second line is the cookie value. The remaining lines define the cookie attributes.

Cookies are most often used to keep track of the client session. Most servers will automatically create a cookie when a new session is created. The cookie will contain the session id and will be set to expire as soon as the client browser has been closed.

In both Servlets and JSPs, cookies are accessed through `HttpRequest`, sent to the client through the `HttpResponse`, and encapsulated as `javax.Servlet.http.Cookie` objects.

CORE CONCEPTS

Building a Cookie

A cookie is simply a single name-value pair wherein both the name and the value are `String` objects. The steps involved in building a cookie are very simple and relate primarily to the cookie configuration. To create a new cookie, simply instantiate the `Cookie` class by passing in both the name and the value.

A `Cookie` may also be configured with one or more characteristics that are set using `setXXXX()` methods:

- Domain—The domain attribute specifies a web domain that should receive the cookie (e.g., www.codenotes.com). By default this property is set to the domain that created the cookie.
- MaxAge—You can set the cookie life span (in seconds). If the value is negative or zero, the cookie will be destroyed when the browser is closed.
- Path—If you set a path attribute, the client will automatically send the cookie to the specified URL. The URL must include the Servlet that created the cookie.
- Secure—If this flag is set to `true`, the cookie will be sent only if a secure protocol such as HTTPS or SSL is available.
- Version—If version is set to 0, the cookie will comply with the original specification. If version is set to 1, the cookie will comply with the newer RFC 2109 specification (www.w3.org/Protocols/rfc2109/rfc2109). You should generally use 0, because browser support for the new-style cookie is very sporadic.

The following example places the name-value pair "Cookie-Monster" on the client browser:

```
//assumes import of javax.servlet.http.*
Cookie myCookie = new Cookie("Cookie", "Monster");
myCookie.setSecure(false);
myCookie.setVersion(0);
myCookie.setMaxAge(60*60*24*7); //one week
//add the cookie to the response object.
res.addCookie(myCookie);
```

Listing 5.19 Creating and configuring a cookie

Reading Cookies

If you have created a cookie for a particular page or set of pages, the client will automatically append the cookie to the HTTP header when it requests the page again. If the cookie has expired, of course, it will not be included.

When a client returns a cookie, you can access it through the `HttpRequest.getCookies()` method. This method returns an array of `Cookie` objects. You can iterate through the array with a simple `for` loop:

```
//assumes a request object called req (in doGet or doPost)
//assumes you have imported javax.servlet.http.*
Cookie[] myCookies = req.getCookies();
for (int i=0; i<myCookies.length; i++) {
  out.println("Cookie name: " + myCookies[i].getName());
  out.println("Cookie value: " + myCookies[i].getValue());
}
```

Listing 5.20 Accessing cookies

Once you have the `Cookie`, you can use the `getXXXX()` methods to extract the name, value, or any of the configuration parameters.

EXAMPLE

NoBannerCookie

Some commercial websites are thoughtful enough to allow you to turn off popup banners with a configuration setting. This setting is the perfect example of a good cookie opportunity. The first code fragment shows the cookie-writing process:

```
//assumes import of javax.servlet.http.*
Cookie myCookie = new Cookie("PopUpBanners", "False");
myCookie.setSecure(false);
myCookie.setVersion(0);
/** Set the path to the banners directory, so all of the banner
pages can read the cookie **/
myCookie.setPath("/banners");
myCookie.setMaxAge(60*60*24*7); //one week
//add the cookie to the response object.
res.addCookie(myCookie);
```

Listing 5.21a The NoBannerCookie example

Of course, the web developer also has to read the cookie and check the value in the page that would create the banners:

```
boolean goBanners = true;
Cookies[] myCookies = req.getCookies();
for (int i=0; i<myCookies.length; i++) {
  if ((myCookies[i].getName().equals("PopUpBanners"))
            && (myCookies[i].getValue().equals("False")))
    goBanners = false;
}
if (goBanners) {
  //build banners
}
```

Listing 5.21b   NoBannerCookie, part two

HOW AND WHY

How Do I Know Whether the Client Has Rejected a Cookie?

Clients do not explicitly reject cookies. Rather, the client simply ignores the cookie when it is sent. No error messages, warnings, or notifications are generated or returned to the browser. On a subsequent HTTP request to the server, a Servlet can check if the cookie exists in the `HttpServletRequest` object. If the `Cookie` does not exist, the client did not retain it. You can also create a client-side JavaScript method to check for the cookie, as illustrated on the CodeNotes website CN `J2050004`.

How Do I Create Cookies with Multiple Values?

The cookie definition specifies a single name-value pair. However, there is nothing that prevents you from concatenating several variables into a single value. This will save you the overhead of building and accessing multiple cookies, but it will cost you in terms of building and using a string parser to separate out the values. Most cookie values comprised of concatenated values use the "&" character as a separator.

BUGS AND CAVEATS

Cookie Security

Cookies by their very nature should be considered unsecure data storage. You have absolutely no control over the cookie environment on the client. Users can easily modify or erase any cookie at any time, including midsession.

Obviously, a cookie should never contain an unencrypted password or any other privileged client data.

DESIGN NOTES

In many cases, you should use the session attributes instead of cookies. Cookies depend on client settings and may slow down your web pages (depending on the number of cookies you must send and receive). Session attributes provide faster page access at the cost of more server resources, especially memory.

The trade-off is the large scalability of cookies versus the data integrity and speed of session attributes. If you are expecting a large number of simultaneous website hits, session attributes may require too much memory, and you will probably need to use cookies.

SUMMARY

Cookies are small key-value pair text files that are stored on the client. You can create and access cookies through the `HttpServletRequest` and `HttpServletResponse` objects. Cookies should be used with care, as security will always be a concern.

Chapter Summary

Servlets are compiled Java classes that act as dynamic web pages. Servlets are easy to build and can provide powerful program flow control.

In the next chapter, you will see an alternative to Servlets that is much more friendly for writing HTML web content. Nevertheless, Servlets provide a valuable Java environment for application code and flow control and will be a part of any large web application.

Chapter 6

JAVASERVER PAGES

The previous chapter, on Servlets, demonstrated the building of compiled Java classes that act as server-side web pages. JavaServer Pages (JSPs) extend this functionality by allowing you to build web pages that are converted to Servlets at runtime. The advantage of JSPs over Servlets is that the outer Servlet framework is still available, yet you can develop HTML and Java interchangeably with rapid turnaround.

Once the HTML has been freed from the confines of pure Java code, development of the web application can proceed along the natural division lines:

- Back-end functionality (Java)—Back-end components can be built and tested as stand-alone Java classes (or EJBs). These classes can be built without any thought to web display or any knowledge of web languages such as HTML, DHTML, or JScript.
- Application functionality (Servlets and/or JSP)—Application controllers or page-specific components can be built as either Servlets or JavaServer Pages.
- Interface and Display (JSP, HTML, XML, etc.)—The purely visual and interactive components can be built with traditional web tools such as HTML, incorporating Java where necessary. The web developers do not necessarily need to know or work with Java.

Although JavaServer Pages and Servlets share many capabilities, JSP is not a replacement for Servlets. In fact, you can think of a JavaServer

Page as a Servlet that has been turned inside-out. The Servlet encapsulates the entire page in a stand-alone Java class. The JSP exposes the raw HTML and encapsulates the Java code in a set of HTML-like tags. Thus, Servlets are better suited to application flow control and JSPs are better suited to the building of interface and display components.

The major caveat to JSPs is that it is relatively easy to create unmaintainable pages with large sections of commingled Java and HTML. Avoiding this situation requires the discipline to move as much Java code as possible out of the interface. Although mixed languages (HTML and Java) can be useful, they also add a layer of potentially confusing syntax and a requirement that a developer be conversant in both languages. Throughout this chapter, you will see how JSP works as a mixed-language technology, but you will also see how to leverage JSP as a means of moving "functional" code out of the "interface and display" code.

Simple Application

This is a simple JavaServer Page. As you will see, JSP technology provides the possibility for rapid HTML development while allowing access to all the Java classes and components. This simple application is the JSP version of the Servlet Hello World application:

```
<html>
<body>
<%String text = "World";
if (request.getParameter("subject") != null)
  {text = request.getParameter("subject");} %>
Hello <%=text%>
</body>
</html>
```

Listing 6.1 A simple JSP application

If you access the page with the basic URL (e.g., hello.jsp), the output will be

```
Hello World
```

However, if you access the page with a URL that has a "subject" parameter (e.g., hello.jsp?subject=CodeNotes%20Reader), the output will be

```
Hello CodeNotes Reader
```

Core Concepts

JSPs share many core concepts with Servlets. Even if you do not plan to use Servlet technology, you should review the core concepts of the Servlets chapter.

PREREQUISITES

As a quick refresher, you should have already done the following:

1. Created a web application directory (called C:\webdev). Whenever you create a JSP, you should put it in this directory.
2. Installed and started Tomcat. To start Tomcat on Windows, you need to open a command window and launch the startup.bat file (e.g., C:\Jakarta\bin\startup.bat). If you are using a different JSP container, make sure it is properly installed, configured, and running.

If you haven't built an application directory or do not know how to install or start the Tomcat server, please refer to Chapter 2 (Installation).

JSP BUILDING BLOCKS

JSP syntax is comprised of four basic building blocks. Each of these blocks contains a set of HTML or XML tags and tools used for adding Java to a web application:

- Scripting Elements—JSPs are built using comments, expressions, scriptlets, and declarations. These are the basic building blocks of JSPs.
- Directives—The three directives, `page`, `include`, and `taglib`, extend the basic scripting capabilities by providing compiler directives, including class and package libraries, and by importing custom tag libraries.

  Custom tag libraries provide XML syntax for accessing external Java code. Tag libraries are an important tool for factoring common scripting elements out of JSPs for improved maintainability. Tag libraries are explained in a series of articles on the CodeNotes website `J2060001`.

- Actions—Actions further extend JSP by providing "forward" and "include" flow control, applet plug-ins, and access to JavaBean components.
- Implicit Objects—Implicit objects are instances of specific Servlet interfaces (e.g., `javax.Servlet.http.HttpServletRequest`) that are implemented and exposed by the JSP container. These implicit objects can be used in JSP as if they were part of the native Java language.

JSP LIFE CYCLE

JavaServer Pages have a slightly different life cycle than Servlets. Servlets are fully compiled Java classes, whereas JSPs must be compiled into Servlets before they can be accessed. This compilation step is handled by the JSP container at runtime. When a JSP is requested, the container looks for a Servlet class. If the class does not exist, or if the Servlet compile date is older than the last access date on the JSP, the JSP is compiled.

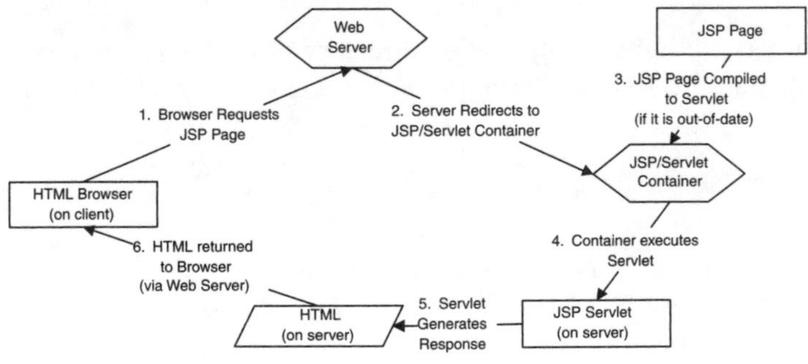

Figure 6.1 A typical JSP life cycle. For the user, steps 2–5 are transparent, while the developer only has to think about the JSP.

In general, the life cycle follows a pattern similar to that of a Servlet, except for the extra step of compiling the JSP. However, this step is handled by the container and is transparent for both developers and web users.

JSP to Servlet Compilation

When a JSP file is accessed, the container converts it into a Java class that implements the `javax.servlet.jsp.HttpJspPage` interface. The various JSP building blocks are translated into Java code and compiled into a Servlet.

Topic: JSP Scripting Elements

This topic explains the basic JSP syntax. At first glance, a JavaServer Page looks much like an ordinary HTML document. Much of the JSP syntax is based on a set of tags very similar to those of HTML or XML. As you read a page of JSP, however, you may notice sections that are pure Java syntax. Using server-side scripting tags, you can encapsulate Java code directly in the web page.

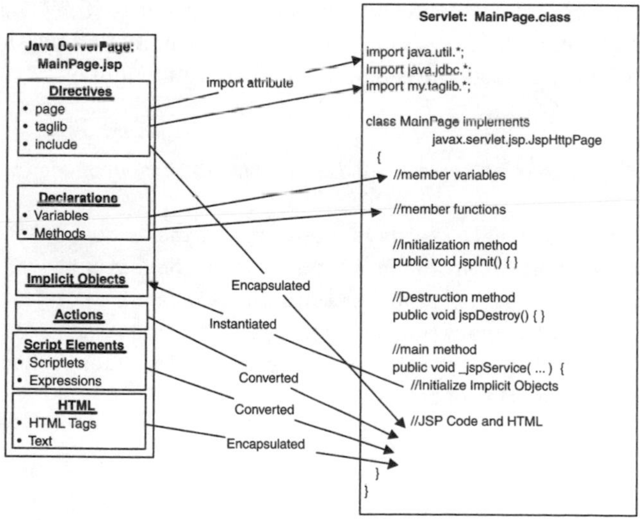

Figure 6.2 The various JSP building blocks are converted to Java code inside the Servlet

This topic will show you the basic syntax for comments, declarations, expressions, scriptlets, and escape characters. Although it sounds complicated, remember that most of this syntax combines basic Java with some specific HTML-like tags that are very easy to use.

CORE CONCEPTS

Comments

There are several ways to comment your JSP code. Some types of comments will be pushed through to the final HTML that is passed to the client, whereas others will not be displayed. Some comment types are ignored when the JSP is converted to a Servlet. These comments are not displayed on the final client-side HTML. Generally, the choice of which form to use comes down to two questions:

1. Do you want the comments to be visible if the client chooses to view the HTML source for the page? If so, use HTML comments.
2. Does the comment format match the current format in your JSP? For example, in a scriptlet section (pure Java), you should use standard Java comments. In an HTML section, you should use HTML comments.

JSP comments can be encapsulated in "<%--" and "--%>" tags, or as regular Java comments inside a code segment, using "<% /**" and "**/ %>" tags. Comments that should be visible in the final client-side code should be encapsulated with standard HTML comment tags: "<!--" and "-->".

```
<%-- This comment will not appear in the HTTP source sent to the
client --%>
<% /** This is a regular Java comment inside a code block. It
will not be sent with the html pushed to the client.  **/ %>
<% //this is a single line comment in a java block.
//These comments are also not sent to the client %>
<!-- Standard HTML comment.  Visible when the client chooses to
view source for the page -->
```

Listing 6.2 Types of comments

Declarations

JSP declarations are equivalent to member variables and functions of a class. The declared variables and methods are accessible throughout the JSP. These declarations are identified by using <%! %> or the XML equivalent <jsp:declaration></jsp:declaration> tags. You can combine multiple declarations in the same set of tags, including combinations of variables and methods.

```
<%-- Declaring a page level String variable --%>
<%! String bookName = "J2EE CodeNote"; %>
<%-- Declaring a page level public method --%>
<%! public String palindrome(String inString) {
  String outString = "";
  for (int i = inString.length(); i > 0; i--) {
    outString = outString + inString.charAt(i-1);
  }
  return outString;
} // palindrome
%>
<%-- Multiple declarations --%>
<%!  int maxCounts = 50;
     double avagadrosNum = 6.02E23;
%>
```

Listing 6.3 Types of declarations

Another use for declarations is accessing the `jspInit()` and `jspDestroy()` life cycle methods. As you will recall from the Life Cycle Concept section, `jspInit()` is called immediately after the JSP Servlet has been instantiated but before any requests are processed. The `jspDestroy()` method is called immediately prior to the Servlet destruction. Both methods are automatically created by the JSP container; however, you can override the default methods and include code that should be called on page initiation or destruction. These methods are rarely used, but they can be very useful for initializing and releasing resource variables such as `javax.sql.DataSource` objects.

```
<%-- Example jspInit() and jspDestroy() methods --%>
<%! public void jspInit() { //Insert code here}
    public void jspDestroy() {//insert code here} %>
```

Listing 6.4 The special life cycle control methods

A Warning

As indicated in Figure 6.2, method declarations are added as independent sections to the code outside of the main `_jspService()` method. As with any Java class, declarations cannot reference any variable or method that has not already been declared. In particular, declared methods cannot take advantage of any of the structure built into `_jspService()`. Within a declared method, you cannot:

- Write HTML directly (using scriptlet tags <% %>).
- Use expressions (described in the next section).
- Use implicit objects (described in the Implicit Objects topic).
- Reference a declared variable or method that was not declared earlier in the JSP.

Although this appears to diminish the utility of declared methods, you can work around most of the limitations by having your declared methods return a `String` value containing HTML text. For example, you might convert an array of strings into a table row using code like this:

```
<%! public String tableRow(String[] cellValues) {
  String tableHtml = "<TR>";
  for (int i=0; i<cellValues.length(); i++) {
    tableHtml += "<TD>" + cellValues[i] + "</TD>";
  }
  tableHtml += "</TR>";
  return tableHtml;
}
```

Listing 6.5a A declared method for writing a table row

Your JSP might use this code as the argument in an expression. The following code fragment illustrates this:

```
<% String[] petNames = {"Spike", "Velcro", "Lady Brillo"};
   String[] petAges = {"3 yrs.", "5 yrs.", "3.5 yrs"};%>
This table lists the names of Hedgehogs I have met and their
age:
<TABLE>
  <%=tableRow(petNames)%>
  <%=tableRow(petAges)%>
</TABLE>
```

Listing 6.5b The JSP that uses the method from Listing 6.5a

Expressions

An expression is an in-line function that writes text to the buffer. Each set of expression tags encloses a fragment of Java code that must evaluate to a `String`. Expressions are enclosed in either <%= %> or <jsp:expression> </jsp:expression> tags. The JSP container will generate compilation errors if your expression cannot be converted into a `String`, or if you have placed a semicolon at the end of your Java statement.

An alternative method for writing to the buffer uses the "out" implicit object, explained in the Implicit Objects topic later in the chapter.

```
<%-- Using the basic expression script tags--%>
<%! String text = "Wow!";%>
This is some html and an expression: <%=text%> </br>
<%-- The same thing using the XML tags--%>
<jsp:declaration>String text = "Wow!";</jsp:declaration> </br>
This is some html and an expression:
<jsp:expression>text</jsp:expression>
<%-- And finally, using the out object --%>
<%! String text = "Wow!";%>
This is some html and an expression: <%out.print(text)%> </br>
```

Listing 6.6 Types of expressions

The script tags are used most often. Nevertheless, there are times when using `out.println()` or `out.print()` makes sense, particularly when you are in the middle of a scriptlet where adding an extra set of <%= %> tags would make the code confusing.

Scriptlets

A scriptlet is a section of Java code embedded in HTML. A scriptlet can include any valid Java code. This means that you can:

- Declare new variables—The variables are "scriptlet" level and cannot be accessed outside of the scriptlet.
- Instantiate external classes—You can access JDBC, RMI, JNDI, or any other package of Java classes from inside a scriptlet, provided you have included the package with the correct directive.
- Access JavaBeans—You can access the properties and methods of a JavaBean inside a scriptlet. Another method for using JavaBeans is covered in the Forms, JavaBeans, and JSP topic later in this chapter.

Scriptlets are declared using the <% %> script tags, or the <jsp:scriptlet> </jsp:scriptlet> XML equivalents.

```
<%-- This is a simple scriptlet --%>
<%! String colors[] = {"red", "green", "blue"};%>
<TABLE>
  <TR>
    <%for (int i = 0; i < colors.length; i++) {
```

```
      out.println("<TD>" + colors[i] + "</TD>");
    }%>
  </TR>
</TABLE>
```

Listing 6.7 Scriptlets

Escape Characters

Every computer language has reserved characters, such as double quote ("), single quote ('), forward slash (/), and the various forms of parentheses ({[]}). When you are working with JSP, you should remember that you are dealing with at least two different sets of reserved characters, HTML's and Java's. Ordinarily, reserved characters do not cause a problem. But, when you need to write a reserved character to the HTML page (for example), you need to preprocess the character with a backslash (\) character. The following table lists some additional escape sequences:

Character Value	Escape Sequence
Backspace	\b
Tab	\t
New Line	\n
Form Feed	\f
Latin 1 Character Set Octal 000–377	\xxx
Double Quote	\"
Single Quote	\'
Backslash	\\
Carriage return	\r
Unicode Character Set (0000–FFFF)	\uxxx

Table 6.1 Common escape characters

EXAMPLE

The following example creates a table of product names and prices:

```
<% // assume I have an arraylist of products. %>
<TABLE>
```

```
<TR>
  <TH>Product #</TH>
  <TH>Product Name</TH>
  <TH>Unit Price</TH>
</TR>
<% Iterator it = products.iterator();
  while (it.hasNext()) {
%>
    <TR>
      <% Product aProduct = (Product) it.next();%>
      <TD><%= aProduct.getProductId()%></TD>
      <TD><%= aProduct.getProductName()%></TD>
      <TD><%= aProduct.getUnitPrice()%></TD>
    </TR>
<% } %>
</TABLE>
```

Listing 6.8 A simple JSP example

HOW AND WHY

When Should I Use Script Tags Instead of XML Tags?

The tags are equivalent. The only critical factor is whether your JSP container supports the XML versions. As a rule, XML tags are easier to read but require more typing.

How Do I Use Regular XML Inside a JSP Page?

First, you can interlink JSP syntax with XML directly. For example:

```
<Book>
  <Series>"<%=request.getParameter("series")%>"</Series>
  <Title>"<%=request.getParamter("title")%>"</Title>
</Book>
```

Listing 6.9 XML in a JSP

Second, you can use both the DOM and SAX XML models inside a JSP. DOM and SAX are beyond the scope of this book, but you can learn more about them in *CodeNotes for XML.*

When Should I Use Declarations for Variables?

While you should use declarations to move functions out of your main HTML page, you should be careful with variables. Depending on the container and the exact circumstances, declared variables may retain memory between each page access. In the following code, for example, the variable "i" will increment each time the page is reloaded, while "j" will always equal 1.

```
<%! int i=0;%>
<%  int j=0; %>
<%  i++;
    j++; %>
<b>i = <%=i%></b><br/>
<b>j = <%=j%></b><br/>
```

Listing 6.10 Declared variables

While this may imply that declared variables maintain scope, you should not use declarations that way. These variables are declared when the container first compiles the JSP and creates the Servlet instance. As long as the container keeps the Servlet alive, the variables will retain memory. However, the container can kill the Servlet instance at any time. In addition, if you are working with distributed servers, you may never know which Servlet instance you are accessing.

BUGS AND CAVEATS

Debugging JSP

Bear in mind that a JSP is compiled into a Servlet by the container before it is displayed in the browser. This can make debugging JSP difficult, as the container may return references to code that is substantially different from the JSP. A few things can help make this easier:

- Some containers provide "probable" line numbers for compilation errors. These line numbers should get you close. However, you should always remember that the container is converting your code to a Servlet, so the line numbers may be off.
- Check your container log files. (On Tomcat, these files are stored in the \logs directory—`c:\Jakarta\logs`). These files will store all sorts of information about compilation and runtime errors (which may not be passed onto the browser). The actual log contents are container-specific, but they usually contain timestamps for Servlet life cycle events.
- `System.out` output is redirected to the console or to a logfile, de-

pending upon the JSP container settings. If you are using Tomcat, this output will be sent to the console where Tomcat is running. You can redirect it to a log file by adding a path attribute to the "tc_log" Logger element in the server.XML config file:

```
<Logger name="tc_log"
  verbosityLevel = "INFORMATION"
  path="logs/tomcat.log"
/>
```

Listing 6.11 Setting Tomcat to log errors

Runtime errors can be difficult to track. Remember that a JSP is an HTML page, so you should feel free to add "Entering loop" comments in order to track down the problem lines. Just don't forget to delete them when you find the bug.

XML Tag Support

As of this writing, support for the XML JSP tags is still inconsistent. Some systems fully support XML tags, whereas others have removed support entirely. For instance, the Tomcat container (version 3.x) does not support the XML JSP tags. Early Tomcat versions had limited support, but this was dropped until the standard stabilized. As of this writing, Tomcat version 4.x is slated to reimplement support for XML JSP tags. Over the next year, more containers should move toward full support for XML tags, and Sun has hinted that future versions of JSP may deprecate the older script tags.

DESIGN NOTES

The basic design pattern for JSP is to use lots of HTML and XML, and very little Java code. You can move code off a JSP in several ways:

- Use method declarations to move code out of the main part of your page. Be careful with variables.
- Write the Java code into class objects, JavaBeans, and Servlets.
- Take advantage of the <jsp:useBean> tags described in the Forms, JavaBeans, and JSP topic.
- Use include directives (discussed in the next topic).

Model-View-Controller

When developing a user interface, it is very important to separate common responsibilities into separate objects. The most common division of responsibility is known as Model-View-Controller (MVC) paradigm, more accurately termed Presentation-Abstraction-Controller (PAC). The components are:

- The Model (Abstraction) represents the underlying application objects that access the database, represent business logic, etc. These objects are typically JavaBeans, EJBs, or regular Java classes.
- The View (Presentation) is responsible for rendering the display. Typically this is a JSP that uses helper objects, data objects, and custom tag libraries.
- The Controller is responsible for controlling application flow and mediating between the abstraction and presentation layers. The controller is typically a Servlet.

The client accesses the controller (Servlet) as the main page, or as the target action of a form submission. The controller in turn accesses the underlying business logic and database code of the abstraction layer and sets various data and helper objects into scoped attributes on the Servlet (JavaBeans, EJBs, Java classes). Finally, the request is redirected to the appropriate view (JSP) using `RequestDispatcher.forward()`.

SUMMARY

This chapter covers everything you need to know in order to build basic JSPs. The key points to remember are:

- There are many ways to perform similar functions. Use the one that is most appropriate for you (e.g., `<%=System.currentTimeMillis()%>` vs. `<%out.println(System .currentTimeMillis());%>`).
- Remember that declarations inside a scriptlet are local to the scriptlet. Page level declarations are declared with <%! %> or <jsp:declaration> </jsp:declaration>.
- Use the XML tags if you can. They make your code more readable and more compatible with the anticipated direction of JSP.

The following sections extend the basic functionality of JSPs and illustrate the use of directives (include, page, etc.), actions (forward, applet, plug-in), implicit objects (`Request`, `Response`, `Session`, etc), and JavaBeans (which make data entry much easier).

Topic: Directives and Actions

Directives and actions extend the basic JSP syntax. Directives are instructions from the JSP to the container that can be used to set the page properties, to import Java classes and packages, and to include external web pages and custom tag libraries. The three directives are:

- Page—The page directive sets the attributes of the page and provides the functionality for importing Java classes.
- Include—The include directive adds modularity to JSP by allowing you to include the contents of external pages in your JSP.
- Taglib—The Taglib directive is used for Custom Tag Libraries. This directive is covered in a CodeNotes web article CN J2060001.

Actions, on the other hand, instruct the container to perform specific tasks at runtime. These actions range from forwarding control to another page to generating a new JavaBean for use in the page. The four types of actions are:

- Forward—This action transfers control to a new web page.
- Include—The include action temporarily transfers control to a new page, performs the actions on the page, includes the output in the original page, and returns control to the original page.
- Beans—Bean actions allow creation and use of JavaBeans inside a JSP. The bean actions are explained in the Forms, JavaBeans, and JSP topic.
- Plug-in—The <jsp:plugin> action is used for working with Java applets. Applets are client-side programs that run on a browser. Applets have generally fallen out of favor and the plug-in action is not covered in this book.

The next sections cover the most important features of the page and include directives and the forward and include actions.

CORE CONCEPTS

Page Directive

The page directive has eleven different attributes that control everything from the scripting language to the classes and packages imported into the page. The general syntax for using a page directive is

```
<%@ page attribute1="value1" attribute2="value2" ...%>
<%-- XML equivalent.  Note that the XML equivalent uses
attributes rather than an open/close tag structure.  --%>
<jsp:directive.page att1="value1" att2="value2" .../>
```

Listing 6.12 Page directives

Except for import, each attribute can be used only once in a page directive. The attribute order is unimportant. The various attributes are summarized in the following table:

Attribute	Value	Default	Purpose
autoFlush	Boolean flag	false	When set to true, buffer automatically flushes when full. Default setting holds content until page is finished.
buffer	Size or false	8kb	Sets size of buffer for holding Page output. Set to false to disable buffer. If false, autoFlush must be true.
contentType	MIME type and character set	text/html; charset= ISO-8859-1	Sets content type and character set for output of page. Usually default, "text/XML,"
			"text/html," or "text/plain." charset is any valid MIME charset.
errorPage	URL	none	Redirects to the specified URL on error. See isErrorPage.
extends	Class name	none	Rarely used. If used, the superclass must implement either the javax.Servlet.jsp.

Attribute	Value	Default	Purpose
			HttpJspPage or javax.Servlet.jsp. JspPage interface.
import	class or package name	none	Used to load external Java classes into your JSP. Identical to the standard "import" command in Java
info	String	none	String value describing page. Used by some containers for generating documentation.
isErrorPage	Boolean flag	false	Indicates whether page is an error page that handles exceptions. Discussed in Implicit Objects section.
isThreadSafe	Boolean flag	true	Set to false when page is not thread safe. The container will process page requests sequentially.
language	Scripting language name	java	Support for other scripting languages. Rarely used. If used, all script inside page must use the same language.
session	Boolean flag	true	Set to false if page does not require session support. This option is discussed with the session implicit object.

Table 6.2 Summary of page directive attributes

The following examples illustrate some common uses for the page directive:

- `import`—Using the `import` directive is just like using "import" in a Java class file. This is the most commonly used page directive. You can import multiple classes and packages by separating the names with a comma.

```
<%@ page import="java.sql.*" %>
<%@ page import="java.util.properties, java.text.*"%>
```

- `contentType`—The `contentType` directive is usually left at the default, unless you are working with different character sets or writing XML content.

```
<%@ page contentType="text/XML" %>
```

- `errorPage`—The `errorPage` attribute will redirect the client to a new JSP when an unhanded exception is thrown. The JSP error page must have the `isErrorPage` directive set to "true."

```
<%@ page errorPage="/webdev/admin/error.jsp" %>
```

- `isErrorPage`—If this attribute is set to `true`, the page can access the exception implicit object. Using implicit objects and error handling are discussed later in this section.

```
<%@ page isErrorPage="true" %>
```

Include Directive

The include directive allows you to modularize your web pages and include the entire contents of one file in another. The include directive can be used any number of times in a JSP. The format is simply:

```
<%@ include file="urltoFile" %>
<%-- XML equivalent, once again, uses attributes instead of
open/close tag --%>
<jsp:directive.include file="urlToFile" />
```

Listing 6.13 The include directive

This directive is often used to develop a set of pages that have common features, such as a header, footer, or logo section. By using include, you can pull the common code out of your JSP and reuse it. If you modify the headers section (for example), the changes will be applied immediately to every page that uses the include directive to add the headers file. Note that the pages included using the include directive do not have to be stand-alone web pages. In fact, the included pages should not have <html> and <body> tags, as some browsers will not handle multiple <html> tags in a single file.

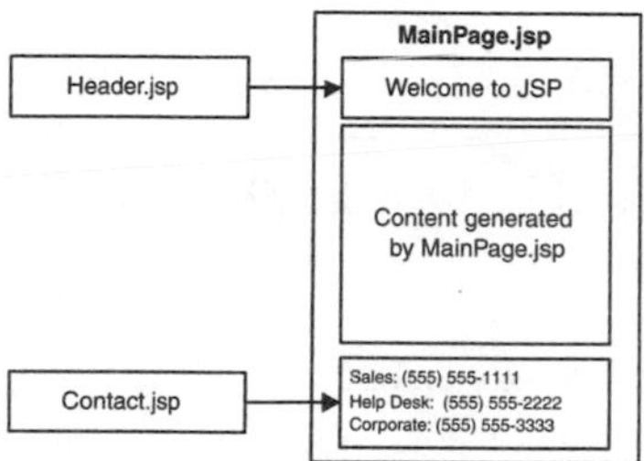

Figure 6.3 You can use the include directive to build multipart JSP pages from common components.

Forward Action

The forward action permanently transfers control to another location using a `RequestDispatcher`. Unlike directives and scripting elements, the forward action does not have a scripting syntax. All actions are launched using an XML syntax:

```
<jsp:forward page="urlToPage" />
```

The forward action supports runtime definition of the page attribute. For example, the following code will forward the page to a URL defined as "msgs/error401.html" if the `errCode` variable is equal to 401:

```
<jsp:forward page='<%= "msgs/error" +errCode+ ".html" %>' />
```

Include Action

Unlike the forward action, the include action temporarily transfers control to another page on the local server. The output of the second page is included in the first page, and control is returned as soon as the second page has finished.

The include action should not be confused with the include directive mentioned earlier. The include action temporarily *transfers* control to the second web page, which must be a complete page. The include directive simply *incorporates* the contents of the second page directly into the calling page.

An include action is called using an XML-based syntax with two attributes, the page URL and "flush." The flush parameter is added for future expansion of the specification. As of JSP 1.1, the flush parameter must be set to "true." This parameter forces the included page to write all of its output before returning control to the calling page.

```
<jsp:include page="urlToPage" flush="true" />
```

This action also supports runtime definition of the page attribute.

Passing Parameters

When you use either the forward or include action, if the receiving page is a JSP, it automatically has access to the `Request` and `Session` implicit objects from the calling page. In practice, this means that the receiving page has access to all of the information passed into the calling page. If you need to pass extra parameters to the receiving page, you can insert <jsp:paramname="*paramname*" value="*paramvalue*" /> into the action. For example:

```
<jsp:forward page="checkout.jsp">
  <jsp:param name="enable" value="true" />
  <jsp:param name="uniqueID" value="<%=uniqueID%>" />
</jsp:forward>
```

Listing 6.15 Passing parameters with forward

These parameters are accessible as form parameters.

EXAMPLES

The following example uses both the include and forward directives to handle a user login scenario. If the user is not logged in, he is automatically redirected to the Login.jsp page.

```
<jsp:include page="/common/Header.jsp"/>
<% String username = session.getAttribute("username");
   if (username == null) {
     // User is not logged in.
```

```
      %> <jsp:forward page="/Login.jsp"/> <%
   } %>
<jsp:include page="/common/Footer.jsp"/>
```

Listing 6.16 A directive example

HOW AND WHY

Should I increase bufferSize or Turn on autoFlush for My Large Pages?

In most cases, the standard settings of `bufferSize` = 8kb and `autoFlush` = "false" will be sufficient. However, when you are building web pages that generate large amounts of data, such as big database queries, you must either increase `bufferSize` or turn on `autoFlush`. The trade-off with `autoFlush` is that once you have sent data to the client, you will not be able to retrieve it. That means that the page may display half of its data and then an exception might occur or a logical condition might force a `<jsp:forward>` action, which could be confusing to the user.

The alternative is to increase the `bufferSize`. This allows you to hold more text in the buffer at the cost of a slower page and larger resource footprint. If it is acceptable for your user to receive a "partial" page, set `autoFlush=true`. Otherwise, increase the page's `bufferSize`. Both properties are attributes of the page directive:

```
<%@ page bufferSize="30kb" autoFlush="false" %>
```

BUGS AND CAVEATS

The Include Directive

The JSP container will automatically recompile a page if the JSP contents are more recent than the compiled Servlet. However, this search does not extend to dependencies, such as files include with the include directive. Whenever you change a file that is referenced in an include directive, you must update the access date on your JSP file in order to force the container to recompile. Otherwise, the included content will not refresh, because the container will use the older compiled Servlet. The Unix "touch" command performs this task nicely. Unfortunately, Windows does not have a direct equivalent. You can update the access date manually by opening the file and saving it. Additionally, there are numerous versions of touchlike shareware programs available for other platforms, such as Windows CN `J2060002`.

DESIGN NOTES

The `import` attribute of the `page` directive is your best friend. Use it to move all application code into Java classes and off your page. Standalone Java classes are much easier to test and debug.

Take advantage of the include directive to incorporate common static HTML elements into your pages. For example, build a simple header file with your logo and contact information. Include the file in all JSP. Any place you have HTML that is repeated between pages, you can use an include directive instead.

SUMMARY

Actions and directives provide valuable extensions to the basic JSP syntax. The most common uses for actions and directives are:

- page import—Use the import attribute of the page directive to include Java classes and packages for use in your page.
- page errorPage—Build a common error page to handle exceptions. Set the "page isErrorPage" attribute to `true` on your error page in order to access the exception object. Error pages are further covered in the Implicit Objects topic.
- include directive—Use the include directive to add small common web components to your programs. This makes your JSP more readable and easier to maintain.
- forward action—Use the forward action to transfer control to a new JSP.

The next topic demonstrates how to access request information, set response information, use the session object, and build error pages.

Topic: Implicit Objects

The JSP container provides access to a set of implicit objects. These objects are extensions of common Servlet components and provide some of the basic tools necessary to build real applications with JSP.

Many of the implicit objects are explained in the Support Objects topic of Chapter 5 (Servlets). In this topic, you will see the JSP-specific aspects of these objects, and several objects that are exclusive to JSPs.

CORE CONCEPTS

Mapping to Servlets

Each of the implicit objects maps to a corresponding class or interface from one of the `javax.Servlet` packages.

Implicit Object	Class
page	javax.Servlet.jsp.HttpJspPage
config	javax.Servlet.ServletConfig
request	javax.Servlet.http.HttpServletRequest
response	javax.Servlet.http.HttpServletResponse
application	javax.Servlet.http.HttpServletContext
session	javax.Servlet.http.HttpSession
pageContext	javax.Servlet.jsp.PageContext
out	javax.Servlet.jsp.JSPWriter
exception	java.lang.Throwable

Table 6.3 Implicit object base classes

The page and config objects are used to access the Servlet that results when the container compiles the JSP. These objects are very rarely used because the various scripting elements, directives, and actions already provide the same functionality.

Overlapping Objects

The most commonly used implicit objects are also the ones that directly overlap with these discussed in Support Objects topic in Chapter 5. `request`, `response`, `application`, and `session` objects are all used just as they are described in the Servlets chapter, except that you do not need the initialization code.

For example, to store attributes in a `session` object, you would use code like this:

```
<%session.setAttribute("number", new Float(42.5));%>
```

To retrieve the parameters from the `request` object, you would use code like this:

```
<%@ page import="java.util.*" %>
<% Enumeration params = request.getParameterNames();%>
```

```
<%while (params.hasMoreElements()) {
    out.print(params.nextElement() + "/t");
  }%>
```

Listing 6.17 Request parameters

Notice that you do not need to instantiate the `out` object. Unlike the case with Servlets, you get the print writer "for free."

As a quick review, the most commonly used features of these objects include:

- Attribute access—Use the `setAttribute()`, `getAttribute()`, and `removeAttribute()` methods on the `session`, `application`, and `request` objects.
- HTTP parameter access—You can access the HTTP header parameters from the request object, and set them on the response object. This includes access to cookies.
- Page flow—You can use the `sendRedirect()`, `encodeURL()`, and `encodeRedirectURL()` methods of the `response` object to redirect the browser to a new page.

Please review the Support Objects topic in Chapter 5 (Servlets) in order to see the detailed explanations of these objects.

PageContext (javax.servlet.jsp.PageContext)

The `PageContext` object is an abstract helper object intended for use by the container. However, the `PageContext` can be used to store attributes (like `session`, `request`, and `application`) in the page scope. The `PageContext` object can also be used to access the other implicit objects (e.g., the `getRequest()` method returns the `Request` object) and perform dispatch methods (forward and include), which are identical to the forward and include actions.

Attributes Revisited

The most useful feature of `PageContext` is that it provides access to all attributes a page can access, regardless of scope. Thus you can use `PageContext` as a one-stop entry point for all of the attributes accessible by the current page.

The extended attribute methods have an extra integer parameter with enumerated values of PAGE_SCOPE, REQUEST_SCOPE, SESSION_SCOPE, and APPLICATION_SCOPE. These scopes relate to the different objects that are capable of supporting attributes. PAGE_SCOPE refers to the `PageContext` object.

- `setAttribute()`, `getAttribute()`, `removeAttribute()`—These methods perform in a manner almost identical to that of the regular methods, with the exception of the added scope parameter.

```
<%//sets Session attribute named "Test"
pageContext.setAttribute("BookTitle", "J2EE",
PageContext.SESSION_SCOPE); %>
```

Listing 6.18 Using the PageContext attribute methods

- `getAttributeNamesInScope(scope)`—This method returns a `Java.util.Enumeration` object with the names (keys) of all of the attributes in the specified scope.
- `findAttribute(key)`—This method searches across all scopes and returns the first instance of the named attribute. The scope search order is: `page`, `request`, `session` (if valid), and `application`. This is very useful if you have a default value (in `application` scope) that can be overridden by a local preference (`session` scope). If no attribute is found, `null` is returned.
- `getAttributeScope(key)`—Returns the scope for the named attribute. If the attribute is not found, this returns an integer value of 0.

You can take advantage of these functions by setting default values in your `application` or `session` object. You can use `PageContext` to iterate through the various scope levels in order to find the lowest-level definition of the attribute. For example, imagine a web search engine that has an optional parameter for the number of results to be returned. You can set a default value in the `application` object and override it locally in the `session` or `request` object. The `PageContext` object can select the value with the narrowest scope.

Out (javax.servlet.jsp.JspWriter)

While the `response` object contains the headers sent to the browser, the `out` object represents the actual output stream and body of the response (i.e., the page buffer). The `out` object extends `java.io.Writer` but incorporates many of the methods from `java.io.PrintWriter`. The `out` object was mentioned in the JSP Syntax topic as an alternative to using the <%=*expression*%> syntax. In fact, the <%=*expression*%> syntax is compiled into "out.print(*expression*);" by the JSP container.

The `out` methods can be grouped into methods for writing to the page buffer and methods for describing the page buffer. Remember that JSPs build HTML on the server and then pass the HTML to the client. The page buffer holds the HTML content until the page has been finished or the buffer has been flushed.

Writing to the Buffer

The `out` object is an implementation of `JspWriter`, which extends `java.io.Writer`. Many of these methods for writing to the buffer should be familiar from standard Java IO access.

- `print()`—Writes data to the buffer, but does not add a line separator.
- `println()`—Writes data to the buffer and adds a line separator.
- `clear()`—Clears the buffer and throws a `java.io.IOException` if data has already been flushed to the client.
- `clearBuffer()`—This is almost identical to `out.clear()`, except that it will not throw an exception if data has already been flushed.
- `newLine()`—This method writes a platform-specific line separator. Using `out.print()` followed by `out.newLine()` is equivalent to using `out.println()`.
- `flush()`—This flushes the output buffer and output stream, sending all of the queued data to the client.
- `close()`—This closes the output stream, flushing any contents. If you use `out.close()`, you will not be able to write any more data to the client from this page.

Describing the Buffer

The out object also supports key methods for describing the current buffer status:

- `isAutoFlush()`—Boolean value indicating whether buffer is automatically flushed when it is filled. By default, this is set to `false`, so an `IOException` will be thrown if the buffer overflows. Remember that you can set this attribute with the page directive:

```
<@ page autoFlush="true" %>
```

- `getBufferSize()`—Returns the buffer size in bytes. If `autoFlush()` is true, it is possible to have a buffer size of 0. You can set the buffer size with the page directive:

```
<@ page bufferSize="12kb" %>
```

- `getRemaining()`—Returns the size of the remaining buffer in bytes.

Exception (java.lang.Throwable)

The exception object is available only on pages that have the `isErrorPage` attribute (from the page directive) set to "true." By default, this value is false, but you can adjust the setting using:

```
<%@ page isErrorPage="true" %>
```

The exception object behaves like a normal `java.lang.Exception`. The most useful methods are:

- `getMessage()`—Returns a string with the descriptive error message (if there is one).
- `printStackTrace()`—Prints the execution stack to the specified buffer.
- `toString()`—Returns a string with the specific class name of the exception and the message. For example: "IOException: File Not Found."

These methods can be combined into a simple error page to which you can direct your other JSPs by using the page directive and the `errorPage` attribute:

```
<%@ page errorPage="util/error.jsp" %>
```

The error page code might look like this:

```
<html>
<%@ page isErrorPage="true" %>
<body>
An unexpected exception occurred: <br/>
<%=exception.toString()%> <br/>
The stack trace is: <br/>
<%exception.printStackTrace(new java.io.PrintWriter(out));%>
```

```
</body>
</html>
```

Listing 6.19 A simple error page

EXAMPLE

The following example uses several of the implicit objects to access and display attributes.

```
<HTML>
<BODY>
<% ProductInformation productInfo = (ProductInformation)
     session.getAttribute("productInfo");
   String requestType = (String)
     request.getAttribute("requestType");
   Integer hitCount = (Integer)
     application.getAttribute("hitCount");
   if (requestType == null || productInfo == null)
     throw new JspException(
       "Invalid request type, or missing information.");
   else if (requestType.equals("Edit")) {
     // Render HTML form for editing productInfo
   } else if (requestType.equals("Read")) {
     // Render HTML table for displaying productInfo
   }
%>
This page has been viewed <%=hitCount%> times since the last restart.
<BODY>
</HTML>
```

Listing 6.20 Implicit object example

HOW AND WHY

Why Don't Servlets Have an Equivalent to PageContext?

The `PageContext` implicit object is a helper class specific to JSPs. All of the `PageContext` methods can be found in the other Servlet helper objects.

Why Can't I Use printStackTrace(out)?

The `printStackTrace()` method is expecting a `java.io.PrintWriter` object, whereas the `out` implicit object is a `javax.Servlet.jsp.JspWriter` object. Even though both classes derive from the same parent class (`java.io.Writer`), `printStackTrace()` will not accept the `out` object. Fortunately, `PrintWriter` accepts a `java.io.Writer` in one of its constructor methods, so we can use the following code:

```
<%exception.printStackTrace(new java.io.PrintWriter(out));%>
```

BUGS AND CAVEATS

Session Attributes

Once again, be careful not to abuse the session attribute objects. The more attributes you add, the more memory the server will require for each user connection.

DESIGN NOTES

HTML, Not Java

Remember that JSP is about lots of HTML and very little Java. Leverage the Model-View-Controller architecture (see the JSP Scripting Elements topic) by moving Java code into helper classes. Use the implicit objects to reduce your Java code even further. It's much easier to read

```
<%session.setAttribute("Good", "JSP");%>
```

than to read

```
<%HttpSession session = request.getSession();
  session.setAttribute("Good", "Servlet style");%>
```

SUMMARY

Implicit objects are helper classes built into the JSP container. These objects provide the glue that ties your JSP together into a single seamless application. Without implicit objects, you cannot easily share data between pages, write to the client, or evaluate the attributes of the client request.

Topic: Forms, JavaBeans, and JSP

Every web page that has data-entry elements such as text boxes or buttons almost certainly uses "form" HTML tags. The form tags encapsulate a set of data entry elements and define the action that occurs when a form is submitted. The HTML for a minimal (nonsecure) login form might look like this:

```
<form action="hello.jsp" method="get" id="form1" name="form1">
  First Name:  <input type="text" name="firstName" /> <br/>
  Last Name:  <input type="text" name="lastName" /> <br/>
  <input type="submit" value="Login"
    id="execute" name="execute" />
</form>
```

Listing 6.21 A basic HTML form

When the user clicks the "Login" submit button, the page will automatically call "hello.jsp" with a QueryString that includes parameters for "login," "password," and "execute." The URL might look like this:

```
hello.jsp?firstName=Lady&lastName=Brillo&execute=Login
```

The hello.jsp page could then access the parameters by using the `request` implicit object with code like this:

```
<% String firstName = request.getParameter("firstName");
  String lastName = request.getParameter("lastName"); %>
Welcome <%=firstName + " " + lastName%>.
```

Listing 6.22 Accessing form values

Although the above example is fairly trivial, imagine the amount of code required to extract all the parameters for a more complicated form such as the registration form for Sun's Java Developers Connection (`developer.java.sun.com/Servlet/RegistrationServlet`), which has fifteen data fields plus a submit button. Worse, you may want to place these values into attributes on your `session` object. This would require at least two lines of code for each and every attribute:

```
String firstName = request.getParameter("firstName");
Session.setAttribute("firstName", firstName);
```

Fortunately, JavaServer Pages provides an alternative in the form of JavaBeans and the <jsp:useBean> action.

JavaBean Refresher

If you have ever worked with Swing, you are intimately familiar with the concept of JavaBeans. A JavaBean is simply a Java class that has member variables (properties) exposed via get and set methods. JavaBeans can be used for almost any purpose, from visual components to data elements. With regards to JSP, JavaBeans are generally data objects, and they follow some common conventions:

- The Java class is named *Something*Bean and should optionally implement the `Serializable` marker interface. This interface is important for beans that are attached to a `session` object that must maintain state in a clustered environment, or if the JavaBean will be passed to an EJB.
- Each bean must have a constructor that has no arguments. Generally, the member variables are initialized in this constructor.
- Bean properties consist of a member variable, plus at least one get method and/or a set method for the variable. Boolean values may use an "is" method instead of get (e.g., `isConfirmed()`).
- The member variables commonly have a lowercase first letter in the first word, with subsequent words capitalized (e.g., firstName). The get and set methods are named get*PropertyName* and set*PropertyName,* where the property name matches the variable name (e.g., getFirstName).
- Get and set accessor methods often perform operations as simple as returning or setting the member variable, but can also perform complex validation, extract data from the database, or carry out any other task that acts on the member variables.

If we created a "UserBean" for the earlier login form example, the code would look like this:

```
package com.codenotes.UserBean;
public class UserBean() {
  private String firstName;
  private String lastName;
  //default constructor
  public UserBean{
    this.firstName = "";
    this.lastName = "";
```

```
  }
  //get methods
  public String getFirstName() {return firstName;}
  public String getLastName() {return lastName;}
  //set methods
  public void setFirstName(String firstName) {
    this.firstName = firstName;
  }
  public void setLastName(String lastName) {
    this.lastName = lastName;
  }
}
```

Listing 6.23 A typical JavaBean

Because of the amount of "pattern code" that is involved in a JavaBean, these classes are almost never written by hand. Most Java development tools, such as Borland JBuilder and IBM VisualAge, have built-in functions for generating accesor methods.

Using JavaBeans in JSP

At this point, you might be wondering why using JavaBeans is any more useful than creating distinct variables in your JSP. You still must use `request.getParameter()` for every property of the form, *and* you must import the UserBean class and create an instance of it (another line of code). However, we can save several lines of code because we only create a single variable ("myBean") rather than a variable for every parameter. Additionally, we need write only a single line of code in order to save the bean as a session attribute:

```
<%com.codenotes.UserBean myBean = new com.codenotes.UserBean;
  myBean.setLastName(request.getParameter("lastName"));
  myBean.setFirstName(request.getParameter("firstName"));
  session.setAttribute("UserBean", myBean);%>
```

Listing 6.24 Using a bean in a scriptlet

While this in itself is a very good reason to use JavaBeans in support of JSPs, the <jsp:useBean> makes this functionality even more powerful.

The Bean Actions

To this point, we have used JavaBeans as we would any other Java class object. However, the <jsp:useBean>, <jsp:getProperty>, and <jsp:setProperty> actions provide a mechanism for treating JavaBeans as if they were HTML components. In fact, these tags provide methods for directly assigning a scope (page, request, session, or application) as well as a means for dumping HTML form data directly to the bean in a single tag statement. Our four lines of code for the UserBean example can be reduced to the following:

```
<jsp:useBean id="UserBean" class="com.codenotes.UserBean"
scope="session"/>
<jsp:setProperty name="UserBean" property="*"/>
```

Listing 6.25 Using the bean action tags

By using these tags, we can reduce our example to two lines of HTML-like code! The advantages are numerous:

1. A large amount of Java code has been deleted, moved off the page, or replaced with HTML-like tags that do not require significant knowledge of Java.
2. The amount of code doesn't change, regardless of the number of properties. Fifteen data fields are handled just as easily as two.
3. Most Java development environments will build the JavaBean code skeleton (variables, get and set methods) automatically. The only code development that is required is defining the bean, building the constructor, and adding data validation.
4. The attributes stored in the page, request, session and application scope can be grouped into JavaBeans, providing quicker, cleaner access. By casting the attribute to the bean, you automatically cast all the properties back to their proper types.
5. Because the JavaBean has standard get and set access methods, you can create a very simple "BeanTestHarness" in order to verify that your bean performs exactly as you expect it to CN J2060003. By isolating the logic in an easy-to-test bean, you can greatly simplify the process of QA testing.

CORE CONCEPTS

Using Beans in Scriptlets

Before diving into the bean action tags, consider how you would use a JavaBean in an ordinary scriptlet. A JavaBean is a compiled Java class, and is treated just like any other object:

```
<%@ import com.codenotes.UserBean; %>
<% UserBean myBean = new UserBean();
   myBean.setFirstName = "Lady";
```

```
  myBean.setLastName = "Brillo";
  out.println("My hedgehog is named " + myBean.getFullName());
%>
```

Listing 6.26 JavaBeans the hard way

UseBean, GetProperty, and SetProperty

The JSP bean tags make the process of creating and using JavaBeans even easier. These three tags perform normal bean operations using an XML syntax that requires almost no knowledge of Java.

<jsp:useBean>

The first and most important tag is <jsp:useBean>, which instantiates a new instance of a JavaBean. The basic tag syntax is:

```
<jsp:useBean id="ObjectName" class="package.objectClass"
  type="package.CastType" scope="BeanScope"
  beanName="nameOfSerializedBean" />
```

- `ID`—The bean `ID` is used to identify the bean throughout its life cycle. The `ID` must be unique and is required in the tag. In essence, this tag creates a new JavaBean variable named by the `ID` attribute.
- `class`—The `class` attribute defines the kind of object that the bean represents. The `class` should contain either a fully qualified package name (e.g., `com.codenotes.UserBean`) or a shortened name if the package has been imported with a `page` directive. This attribute is also required.
- `type`—The `type` attribute is rarely used. Normally, the `useBean` tag creates the bean as an instance of the class defined by the `class` attribute. If the type attribute is present, the bean will be cast to the type specified in this attribute. This can be useful if you need to reference a bean by its base class, or by an interface that the bean implements.
- `scope`—The `scope` attribute assigns the bean to a particular scope. The values for this parameter can be `page`, `request`, `session`, or `application`. If the `scope` tag is omitted, the bean is automatically assigned to the page.
- `beanName`—The `beanName` attribute is used to access a serialized instance of the bean. If this tag is present, the JSP container will pass the `beanName` value to `java.beans.Bean.instantiate()`, which will try to recover the bean from its serialized file. If the

file cannot be found, a new instance of the bean will be created. An example with this attribute can be found on the CodeNotes website CN J2060004.

In some cases, you will want to initialize the bean with key property values as it is created. The <jsp:useBean> tag can be modified to incorporate <jsp:setProperty> tags. These tags are discussed in the next section. The format for initializing a bean with property values is:

```
<jsp:useBean id="myBean" class="com.codenotes.UserBean">
  <%-- initialize with <jsp:setProperty> tags --%>
</jsp:useBean>
```

Several examples of this method are shown in the Examples section of this chapter.

<jsp:setProperty>

Bean properties can be set using <jsp:setProperty>. This tag has three attributes and some hidden functionality (described in the Request Object and Bean Properties section, below) that is particularly useful for web pages.

```
<jsp:setProperty name="BeanId" property="PropertyName"
  value="value" />
```

- `name`—The `name` attribute identifies which bean to access. This attribute references the `id` attribute set in the <jsp:useBean> method.
- `property`—The JSP compiler will add "set" to the property value in order to determine which method to execute. In a special case (described in the Request Object and Bean Properties section) you can set the property value to "*".
- `value`—The `value` attribute holds the value that will be passed into the bean. In some special cases (described in Request Object and Bean Properties), you can omit the `value` attribute.

The `setProperty` tag can be used anywhere on a page, provided that the bean has been created and is in scope. The tag can also be used inside the initialization block of a <jsp:useBean> tag.

<jsp:getProperty>

Once you have created a bean and set its properties, you can access the properties with <jsp:getProperty>. This tag is the simplest tag and has two attributes:

```
<jsp:getProperty name="BeanId" property="PropertyName" />
```

- name—The name attribute is identical to the <jsp:setProperty> name attribute and identifies which bean to access.
- property—The JSP container will add "get" to the property attribute value to determine which method to call on the bean.

This tag can be used anywhere if the referenced bean has been instantiated and is in scope. For example, if a UserBean is instantiated with "session" scope on a login page, the bean properties can be accessed using <jsp:getProperty> on any page that has access to the session.

Request Object and Bean Properties

The omission of the value attribute will tie the <jsp:setProperty> tag directly to the request implicit object. The JSP will scan through the request object for parameter names that match exactly the bean parameter names (remember, it's case-sensitive!). If a match is found, the value from the request parameter will automatically be inserted into the matching bean parameter. Using a tag like

```
<jsp:setProperty name="UserBean" property="FirstName" />
```

is roughly equivalent to using this line of scriptlet code:

```
<% UserBean.setFirstName= request.getParameter("FirstName");%>
```

If you replace the property name with an "*", the JSP will search through all the request attributes and load any attribute that matches. In other words, you can dump the contents of a form directly to a JavaBean if the element names of the form match exactly the property names of the bean. The equivalent Java code involves introspection and a scan through all the request object parameters CN J2060005.

Using Beans in Scriptlets Revisited

Once a bean has been declared by <jsp:useBean>, it can be accessed in a scriptlet as a valid variable, provided the bean is in scope. For example, the following code is perfectly legal:

```
<jsp:useBean id="myBean" class="com.codenotes.UserBean"
  scope="session"/>
<%myBean.setFirstName="Lady";
  myBean.setLastName="Brillo";%>
```

Listing 6.27a Combining the bean actions and scriptlets

In fact, because the bean has session-level scope, we can access the bean in an expression or scriptlet on an entirely different web page (provided the page is in the same session):

```
<html>
  <body>
    My hedgehog is named:
    <%=myBean.getFirstName + "  " + myBean.getLastName %>
  </body>
</html>
```

Listing 6.27b Using the bean in an expression

EXAMPLE

This example fills a form on a JSP using the contents of a JavaBean that was created from an HTML form like this:

```
<FORM>
  First name: <INPUT NAME="firstName" TYPE="TEXT">
<BR>
  Last name:  <INPUT NAME="lastName" TYPE="TEXT">
<P><INPUT TYPE="SUBMIT">
</FORM>
```

Listing 6.28a The form definition

The following code defines the JavaBean in a file called NameBean.java:

```
package com.codenotes.j2ee.jsp;
```

```
public class NameBean implements java.io.Serializable {
  String firstName;
  String lastName;
  public String getFirstName() {
    return firstName;
  }
  public String getLastName() {
    return lastName;
  }
  public void setFirstName(String firstName) {
    this.firstName = firstName;
  }
  public void setLastName(String lastName) {
    this.lastName = lastName;
  }
}
```

Listing 6.28b The JavaBean class

Finally, create the JSP that will use the bean:

```
<jsp:useBean id="nameBean"
    class="com.codenotes.j2ee.jsp.NameBean" scope="session"/>
<jsp:setProperty name="nameBean" property="*"/>
<HTML>
  <BODY>
    Form elements:<P>
    First name: <jsp:getProperty name="nameBean"
    property="firstName"/>
    <BR>
    Last name: <jsp:getProperty name="nameBean"
      property="lastName"/>
    </P>
  </BODY>
</HTML>
```

Listing 6.28c The JSP

HOW AND WHY

How Do I Access Index Properties?

Quite often, you will find a need for an indexed property in a JavaBean. These properties are used to extract a single element of a `Collection`, `array`, or `List`. Usually, these properties have get methods that accept an integer value. Unfortunately, the <jsp:getProperty> and <jsp:setProperty> methods do not support indexed properties because the tags cannot accept the extra parameters. However, you can always access these properties inside a scriptlet:

```
<%-- ShoppingCart is an instance of ShoppingCartBean and has
method getItem(int i) that returns an ItemBean--%>
<% ItemBean newItem = ShoppingCart.getItem(1); %>
```

Listing 6.29 Index properties

Can I Use Enterprise JavaBeans with JSP?

EJBs are discussed in detail in Chapter 8 (Enterprise JavaBeans). Generally, EJBs are not directly accessed from JSP pages using the JSP tags. EJBs are JavaBeans, but they have a different purpose and a different support structure. The most common practice for using EJBs with JSP is to work with regular JavaBeans in JSP and push the data to EJBs from inside the JavaBean. Although this sounds like a roundabout way to code, it does preserve the main principle of JSP, which is the separation of user interface code from application code. It also provides a nice entry point for validation code.

Can I Use Introspection Inside a JSP?

Introspection is the Java term for "holding up a mirror" to a JavaBean in order to determine its properties. For example, you can use introspection inside a JSP to create table headers from the bean properties. An example is provided on the CodeNotes website CN J2060006.

BUGS AND CAVEATS

The Property Wildcard

Consider the following scenario: in an e-commerce site, PurchaseItem.jsp contains a data entry form for purchasing an item and calls BuyItem.jsp. Inside BuyItem.jsp, <jsp:setProperty name="BuyItem" property="*"> is used to dump the product ID, quantity, and unit cost to a BuyItemBean. BuyItem.jsp calculates a "TotalCost" property, which is also set on the BuyItemBean. Normally, this scenario will work fine. But what if someone manually calls BuyItem.jsp with this URL?

```
BuyItem.jsp?Id="123A"&Qty="30"&Cost="23.34"&TotalCost="0.00"
```

Unless the developer has thought to trap invalid TotalCost parameters, the user might just have bought thirty items for zero dollars.

The moral of the story is that you must be careful with the wildcard property dump. If your JavaBean has a set method that matches a property name listed in the QueryString, the JSP will dump the data into that property, whether or not you want it to do so.

DESIGN NOTES

Data Validation

Where should you perform data validation? You can use JavaScript (not discussed in this book) to validate on the client-side, or you can validate the data on the server-side in a JSP, Servlet, JavaBean, or Java class module. Each method has advantages and disadvantages:

- Client-side with JavaScript—The drawback to JavaScript is that you depend on the client's browser to perform important validation tasks. Generally, you should limit this type of validation to simple checks such as data type. The advantages are that JavaScript is fast and that the data is checked before it is submitted to the server.
- Data beans or EJBs—Putting validation code directly in a data bean is generally a bad idea. Validation code slows down retrieval, updates, and inserts. It also creates a hard coupling between your data model and your application interface. You can't modify your data model without drastically altering your interface.
- Validation bean—Creating a separate validation bean is generally a good idea for server-side validation. Use the validation bean until all the data is correct, and then dump the validation bean into an EJB data bean. Validation beans also loosen the coupling between interface and data model. If the data model changes, simply redirect the validation data to a different bean. The main business methods do not change. See the CodeNotes website for an example of this type of validation CN J2060007.

SUMMARY

A JavaBean is simply a Java class that has get and set methods for its member variables. These variables and access methods are called properties. In general, JavaBean code is automatically generated by a Java development environment. JSPs take the use of JavaBeans one step further by providing methods for accessing beans as if they were HTML tags.

Chapter 7

ENTERPRISE JAVABEANS

At the most basic level, Enterprise JavaBeans (EJBs) are simply RMI objects. However, the EJB concept expands beyond traditional distributed computing by placing EJBs in the controlled runtime environment of an application server that provides a rich set of services, such as object pooling, database access, role-based security, and transactional control.

The mechanics of EJBs and the benefits of the application server and EJB container will be illustrated throughout this chapter.

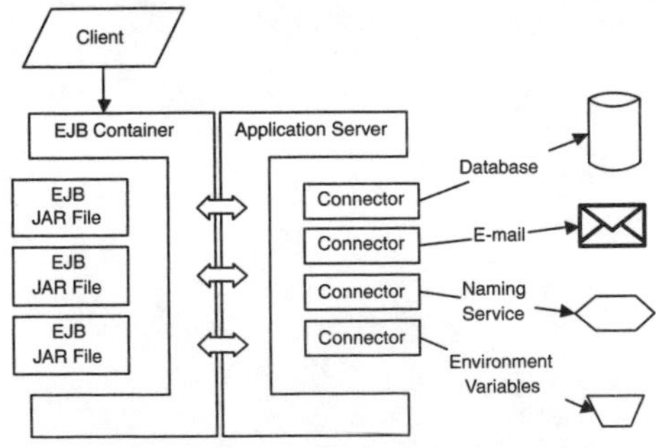

Figure 7.1 An EJB overview

The EJB Application Server and EJB Container

The benefit of Enterprise JavaBeans over other proprietary application server systems is that the EJB framework and runtime environment can be configured declaratively through simple XML files. In other words, the developer is free to concentrate on building business methods and application logic while the server transparently provides commonly used services such as security and transaction control. The infrastructure details are taken care of by the EJB container and application server.

The application server (or J2EE server) provides access to all enterprise services (JDBC, RMI, JNDI, etc.), security, transactions, multithreading, and many other features. The EJB container maps the server interfaces to the actual EJB objects and provides access methods for clients.

Enterprise JavaBeans

Working with EJBs is much like working with RMI objects. However, there are some important differences. Most notably, the EJB model combines aspects of traditional RMI with the object factory pattern. Building an EJB requires two interfaces (`EJBHome` and `EJBObject`) and an implementation class. When you connect to an EJB, you request the reference from the home interface (the factory). Once you have the reference, you can make method calls against the object interface. With normal RMI, you had to provide the connection between the interface and the implementation. However, with EJBs, the EJB container auto-

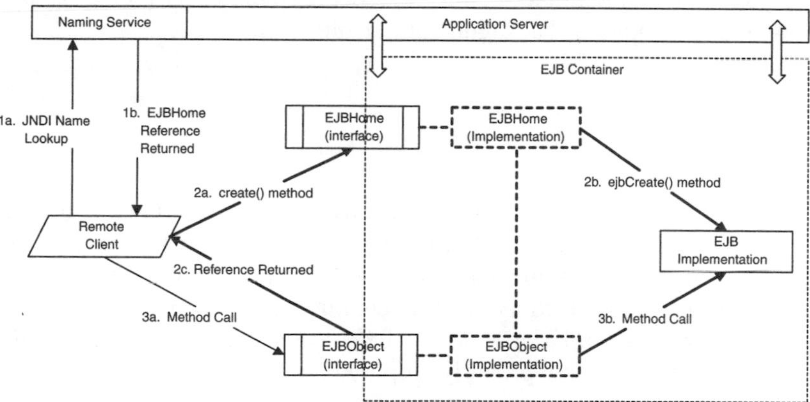

Figure 7.2 A typical EJB. Dashed lines represent container communication or container-built objects.

matically handles the implementation and communication steps. This process is illustrated in Figure 7.2.

A client first connects to the `EJBHome` interface through a JNDI name lookup (Step 1). Then the client executes a `create()` method against the `EJBHome` object. The container takes over, creates an implementation instance and an `EJBObject` instance, and returns a reference to the `EJBObject` (Step 2). Finally, the client executes a method against the `EJBObject`. Once again, the container intercepts the call and issues the command to the EJB implementation, which executes the method (Step 3).

Note that by intercepting the calls to the EJB, the container performs a significant amount of work for you. Because of this interception, the container can insert security and transactional control at runtime. These additional interception actions are configured during the EJB deployment.

Deploying an EJB involves packaging the bean into an EJB-JAR and placing it inside a J2EE Enterprise Archive (EAR). Both of these packaging steps require deployment descriptor files, which are discussed throughout this chapter and in detail in Chapter 8 (Packaging and Deployment). The EJB creation process is illustrated in the Simple Application below.

Caveats

Before you begin this chapter, you should have a good grounding in JDBC, RMI, and JNDI. If you are unfamiliar with these concepts, please read through Chapters 3 and 4 before continuing. This chapter is also very closely tied with the security and deployment descriptor concepts detailed in Chapter 8 (Packaging and Deployment).

Simple Application

The following reusable calculator is a bare-bones example of an EJB stateless session bean. A stateless session bean is a bean that has no memory and stores no information from one method call to the next.

While the code itself is simple, creating and deploying a bean is a multistep process. Even a simple EJB application must be an RMI-compatible object and properly deployed inside an EJB application server. As you are working through this example, it may be helpful to refer to Figure 7.2.

Step 1. Create the Home Interface

The home interface is responsible for creating and removing EJB objects. Think of the home interface as equivalent to an EJB factory. The basic home interface needs to define a zero-argument `create()` method (default constructor). The home interface must extend `javax.ejb.EJBHome`, and throw both `javax.ejbCreateException` and `javax.rmi.RemoteException` on the `create()` methods. Home interfaces are normally named *BeanNameHome* (e.g., CalculatorHome). The EJB container will automatically generate the implementation for this interface when the bean is deployed to the server. The following code should be in a file called CalculatorHome.java, and this file should then be compiled into a class file using javac.:

```
import javax.ejb.EJBHome;
import javax.ejb.CreateException;
import java.rmi.RemoteException;
public interface CalculatorHome extends EJBHome {
  public Calculator create()
    throws CreateException, RemoteException;
}
```

Listing 7.1 The home interface

Step 2. Create the Object Interface

The `EJBObject` interface (sometimes referred to as an object interface) is like any other RMI remote object interface. This interface contains the method prototypes for all the functions you will implement inside the actual bean. As such, the interface serves as a contract describing how any client can interoperate with the bean. Once again, the interface is very simple and contains no implementation code. The object interface must extend `javax.ejb.ejbObject` and throw `java.rmi.RemoteException` on every method. These interfaces are normally named *BeanName* (e.g., Calculator). The following code should be placed in a file named Calculator.java and then compiled into Calculator.class:

```
import javax.ejb.EJBObject;
import java.rmi.RemoteException;
public interface Calculator extends EJBObject {
  public long add(int x, int y) throws RemoteException;
  public long subtract(int x, int y) throws RemoteException;
}
```

Listing 7.2 The remote interface

Step 3. Create the Implementation

The implementation code contains the actual business methods for the bean. The implementation class must implement `javax.ejb.SessionBean`, including providing an implementation of the `ejbActivate()`, `ejbPassivate()`, `setSessionContext()`, `ejbCreate()`, `ejbPostCreate()`, and `ejbRemove()` callback functions. Even if these functions perform no actions, they must be declared. Implementation classes are generally named *BeanName*Bean (e.g., CalculatorBean).

The implementation class does not explicitly need to implement the home or remote interfaces. The EJB container will intercept all calls on those interfaces and forward them to the implementation class. All EJB container callbacks are prefaced with "ejb" to reinforce the relationship between client, container, and class.

The following code should be in a file named CalculatorBean.java and compiled into CalculatorBean.class:

```
import javax.ejb.SessionBean;
import javax.ejb.SessionContext;
public class CalculatorBean implements SessionBean {
  // SessionBean implementation.
  public void ejbActivate() { }
  public void ejbPassivate() { }
  public void setSessionContext(SessionContext ctx) { }
  public void ejbCreate() { }
  public void ejbPostCreate() { }
  public void ejbRemove() { }
  // Calculator methods
  public long add(int x, int y)
  {return x + y;}
  public long subtract(int x, int y)
  {return x - y;}
}
```

Listing 7.3 The implementation

Step 4. Package the Bean

The next steps are to create an XML deployment descriptor for the Bean and build the JAR file that will contain the bean. The deployment descriptor content is described in detail in Chapter 8 (Packaging and Deployment), as is the actual process for creating a JAR file. The basic deployment steps are demonstrated here so that you can deploy and test this example.

To package, deploy, and test this bean, you need the following elements:

1. Calculator.jar—This JAR file will contain CalculatorHome .class, Calculator.class, and CalculatorBean.class from Steps 1–3. This JAR file should also have a subdirectory named META-INF. An EJB deployment descriptor (ejb-jar) will be placed in this directory.
2. CalculatorApplication.ear—This EAR file will contain Calculator.jar and a META-INF subdirectory. Two deployment descriptors (application.xml and sun-j2ee-ri.xml) will be placed in this directory. These descriptors configure the application and provide vendor-specific information for the application server.

To complete Step 1, you need to create the Calculator.jar file. The class files were compiled in Steps 1 through 3. The descriptor file identifies and configures the Calculator EJB. Create a file called ejb-jar.xml and add the following descriptor:

```
<?xml version="1.0"?>
<!--Remove all linebreaks in !DOCTYPE -->
<!DOCTYPE ejb-jar PUBLIC
  "-//Sun Microsystems, Inc.//DTD Enterprise JavaBeans 1.1//EN"
   "http://java.sun.com/j2ee/dtds/ejb-jar_1_1.dtd">
<ejb-jar>
  <enterprise-beans>
    <session>
      <ejb-name>Calculator</ejb-name>
      <home>CalculatorHome</home>
      <remote>Calculator</remote>
      <ejb-class>CalculatorBean</ejb-class>
      <session-type>Stateless</session-type>
      <transaction-type>Container</transaction-type>
    </session>
  </enterprise-beans>
</ejb-jar>
```

Listing 7.4 The ejb-jar deployment descriptor

You now need to build a JAR named Calculator.jar. A more detailed description of this process can be found in the Java Archive section of Chapter 8 (Packaging and Deployment). For this simple example, create a directory (e.g., C:\calculator) and place CalculatorHome.class, Calculator.class, and CalculatorBean.class into this directory. Then create a subdirectory named META-INF (e.g., C:\calculator\META-INF) and copy ejb-jar.xml into it. This directory name must be in upper case. Using a console window, use CD to navigate so that you are in the directory at the same level as the class files, one level above META-INF (C:\calculator). Use the jar command ($JAVA_HOME\bin\jar) to compress the directory into a jar file:

```
jar cf Calculator.jar *
```

You will now have a file called Calculator.jar. Step 1 of deployment is completed. If you opened this file with a zip utility such as WinZip, you would see the following hierarchy:

```
\CalculatorHome.class
\Calculator.class
\CalculatorBean.class
\META-INF\ejb-jar.xml
```

Step 5. Package the Application

This step is generally performed after all EJBs, application-clients, and web applications are built and packaged. For the purposes of this example, you will create a very simple enterprise application and deploy it on the J2EE reference implementation. Once again, many of these steps are revisited in greater detail in Chapter 8 (Packaging and Deployment).

The first step is to create a deployment descriptor for the application. This descriptor identifies all of the components (EJBs, Web Archives, application-clients) that make up the enterprise application. Create an XML file named "application.xml":

```
<?xml version="1.0"?>
<!--Remove all linebreaks in !DOCTYPE -->
<!DOCTYPE application
  PUBLIC "-//Sun Microsystems, Inc.//DTD J2EE Application 1.2//EN"
  "http://java.sun.com/j2ee/dtds/application_1_2.dtd">
<application>
  <display-name>CalculatorApplication</display-name>
  <description>A simple calculator.</description>
  <module>
    <ejb>Calculator.jar</ejb>
  </module>
</application>
```

Listing 7.5 The application deployment descriptor

Each application server requires vendor-specific information in one or more additional deployment descriptor files. Since our vendor in this case is Sun and we are using the J2EE reference implementation, you will need to create a file named sun-j2ee-ri.xml, which must contain the following:

```
<?xml version="1.0"?>
<j2ee-ri-specific-information>
  <server-name></server-name>
  <rolemapping />
  <enterprise-beans>
    <ejb>
      <ejb-name>Calculator</ejb-name>
      <jndi-name>Calculator</jndi-name>
    </ejb>
  </enterprise-beans>
</j2ee-ri-specific information>
```

Listing 7.6 The reference implementation deployment descriptor

The next step is to package the Calculator. jar file and the deployment descriptors in an EAR file. Again, detailed instructions for creating an EAR file can be found in the Enterprise Application Deployment section of Chapter 8 (Packaging and Deployment). The EAR file (CalculatorApp.ear) is really just another JAR file that will contain Calculator.jar and, in a subdirectory named META-INF, the two XML files shown above (application.xml and sun-j2ee-rmi.xml). The internal directory structure of the EAR file should be as follows:

```
\Calculator.jar
\META-INF\application.xml
\META-INF\sun-j2ee-r1.xml
```

To create this EAR file, it is easiest to create a new directory (C:\calculatorapp), copy Calculator.jar into it, create a subdirectory called META-INF (C:\calculatorapp\META-INF), and copy application.xml and sun-j2ee-ri.xml into META-INF. Then, after navigating to your parent directory (C:\calculatorapp), type:

```
jar cf CalculatorApp *
```

Now you are ready to deploy your new Calculator EJB.

Step 6. Deploy the Application

To deploy this application to the Sun J2EE reference implementation server, first start up the server with the J2EE command, which can be found in the $J2EE_HOME/bin directory (e.g., C:\j2sdkee1.2.1\bin\j2ee.bat).

Then use the deploytool to perform the actual deployment:

```
deploytool -deploy CalculatorApp.ear localhost
CalculatorClientLibrary.jar
```

Listing 7.7 Deploying the application

This deploys the modules inside CalculatorApp.ear on the server address localhost and builds a client library called CalculatorClientLibrary.jar. The client library contains the interfaces and RMI stubs required for a client to communicate with the EJB. You need to copy this file to the client machine (if different from where the J2EE server is running) and add this JAR file to the client machine's CLASSPATH.

Step 7. Building a Client

In order to connect to the CalculatorBean, your client must have both the client library (CalculatorClientLibrary.jar) and the j2ee.jar in the CLASSPATH. Create a simple client named CalcClient.java:

```
import javax.rmi.PortableRemoteObject;
import javax.naming.InitialContext;
public class CalcClient {
  public static void main(String[] args) throws Exception {
    CalculatorHome calcHome = lookupCalculatorHome();
    Calculator calculator = calcHome.create();
    System.out.println("3 + 4 = " + calculator.add(3, 4) );
    System.out.println("3194 - 2832 = "
      + calculator.subtract(3194, 2832) );
    calculator.remove();
  }
  public static CalculatorHome lookupCalculatorHome()
           throws Exception {
    InitialContext ic = new InitialContext();
    Object calculatorReference = ic.lookup("Calculator");
```

```
    return (CalculatorHome)PortableRemoteObject.narrow(
      calculatorReference, CalculatorHome.class);
  }
}
```

Listing 7.8 Building an EJB client

Before you run the client, make sure that the reference implementation is running on your server (j2ee.bat or j2ee.sh).

CORE CONCEPTS

The following core concepts illustrate why EJBs are so different from normal Remote Procedure Call frameworks such as RMI, CORBA, and COM. However, if you are interested in the mechanics of how to create EJBs, you can skip ahead to the Basic Beans topic and return to these concepts after you have seen EJBs in action.

Session Beans and Entity Beans

In many ways, EJBs look and act like regular RMI objects. However, a big difference is that EJBs conform to a very specific design pattern, while RMI objects are free-form. The EJB specification defines two types of bean (session and entity), each of which has two flavors. All four bean types will be discussed later in this chapter.

Session Beans

Session beans are the workhorses of the EJB specification. Each session bean acts as a helper class, encapsulating a specific set of business methods. Most session beans are "stateless" and do not retain memory between method calls. Stateless session beans are the most common type of EJB and are used for "fire and forget" methods. A client accesses the bean and uses it to perform specific tasks, such as updating data, performing a calculation, or generating a report. The Calculator example, earlier in the chapter, is a simple stateless session bean.

In some cases, the client needs to perform more complicated tasks that require memory storage between calls. The second variety of session bean, the stateful bean, is specifically designed to provide memory storage for a single client at a time. These stateful session Beans act like conversational agents, allowing a client to perform multiple methods on the same set of data.

While you can design a fairly complicated system using nothing but stateless and stateful session beans, these Beans are inherently tied to a single client and are designed for short-term or transient use. When you have an object that should be shared between clients (such as a representation of database data), you should consider entity beans.

Entity Beans

Unlike session beans, entity beans are designed as permanent representations of data. Entity beans are not tied to any particular client and must be accessed by a unique identity, or primary key. Each entity bean represents a unique set of data (usually drawn from a database). Entity beans have a longer life cycle than session beans and can be accessed by many clients.

Where session beans deal with state, or retaining memory between client calls, entity beans deal with persistence, or retaining memory permanently. The first variety of entity beans uses Bean-Managed Persistence (BMP), which means that the developer has to generate all of the code to provide persistence. Typically, this means you have to write lots of SQL calls to a database.

The second flavor of entity beans uses Container-Managed Persistence (CMP). Because the calls needed to provide persistence are fairly redundant, some EJB containers provide object-relational mapping tools that let you couple the entity bean to a database without writing the actual SQL code yourself. While this may seem like a simple and very useful concept, it actually involves some subtle design issues and requires experienced developers and good tools.

Both types of entity beans are generally used for coarse-grained representation of database data. You will rarely find the need to write a bean to represent a single row in a single table.

Beans in Practice

A typical EJB application will use stateless session beans, stateful session beans, and either CMP or BMP entity beans in combination to provide a rich and varied set of services for web applications and application-clients.

The EJB Container

As illustrated in Figure 7.1, EJBs exist inside a container, which is intimately connected with the application server. The application server (also called J2EE server) provides access to external resources as well as a framework for security and transactional control. The EJB container is the adapter between the application server's internal interfaces, the client, and the EJB.

The EJB container provides "contracts" for three types of functionality:

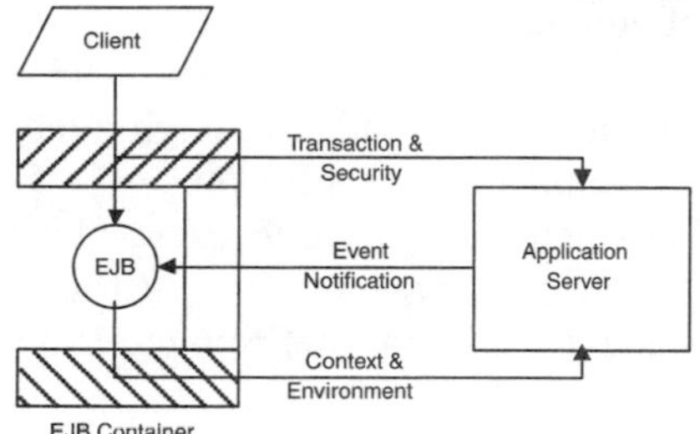

Figure 7.3 The relationship between the container, server, EJB, and client. The shadings on the container represent automatic services, event notification, and programmatic services.

1. Automatic Services. The container handles basic security and transactional services through interceptor objects and deployment descriptors. These are known as automatic services because they are configured declaratively at deployment time.
2. Event Notifications. The EJB container provides event notification to EJBs through a callback interface.
3. Programmatic Services. EJBs can access environment settings through context objects. Environment settings eliminate the need to hard-code initialization settings and resource names in the EJB. These settings are stored in the container and defined through the deployment descriptor.

All three of these contracts are discussed in greater detail in the following sections.

Automatic Services and Interceptors

Traditional application servers expose services such as transaction and security control through a proprietary API. J2EE servers, on the other hand, work through a configuration file. Because of this, most basic services can be declaratively configured instead of programmed. The common automatic services include:

- Transaction demarcation—The server provides built-in methods for transaction creation, commit, and rollback functions.
- Role-based method level security—J2EE servers have a built-in security model. This model can provide method-level security on an EJB at deployment time.
- Database schema—With entity beans and Container-Managed

Persistence, the server can actually expose the persistent database schema of your business components.

These transparent services are provided through interceptor objects that are part of the EJB container. An interceptor object handles all client calls to EJB methods and transparently inserts the necessary service API calls to the underlying EJB server. To illustrate the difference between this process and more traditional Remote Procedure Calls (such as RMI), consider Figure 7.4:

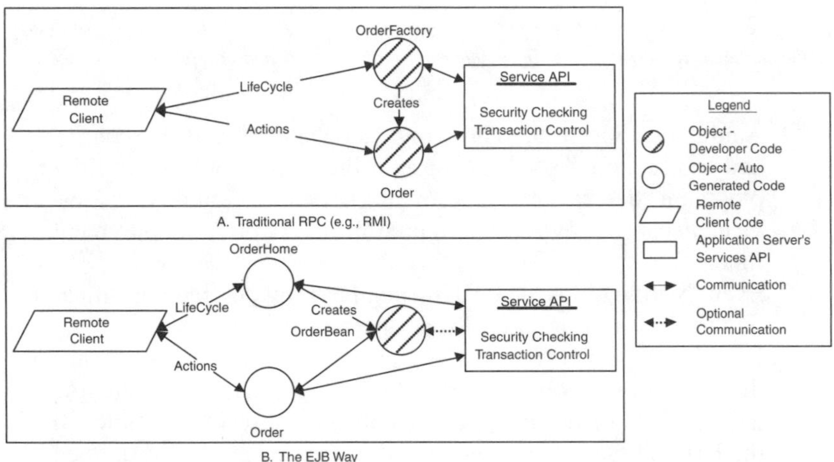

Figure 7.4 Traditional RPC vs. EJB

With traditional RPC, the developer is required to implement business logic, life cycle management, and calls to the service API. Every single object will require some of this overhead code that crosscuts through all the objects.

With EJBs, these crosscutting methods are moved out of source code and into a declarative configuration file, thus saving a significant amount of development. While this means that EJB is more complex than traditional RPC with an application server, most of the complexity is hidden from the developer. The developer builds two interfaces that extend `EJBHome` and `EJBObject`, which the container implements as interceptor objects, shown in subdiagram B above. These interceptors delegate remote calls to the EJB implementation class, but first insulate the EJB implementation class from the mechanics of security checking, transaction control, and remote communication.

Event Notification

The runtime model of RMI is changed by EJB to facilitate the management of large numbers of object instances in memory. The most important change deals with callbacks. When the container detects certain events, it executes the callback method in the EJB implementation class. You can use these callbacks to make your bean respond to runtime actions.

All callbacks except `ejbCreate()` and `ejbFind()` are defined in the `SessionBean` or `EntityBean` interfaces. The most common callback methods are:

- `ejbCreate()`—This method fires when the bean is created.
- `ejbPostCreate()`—This method fires immediately after the bean is created. This method is most often used with stateful session beans and entity beans.

  Both an `ejbCreate()` and an `ejbPostCreate()` method must be defined in the implementation code for every `create()` method declared on the EJB's home interface.
- `ejbPassivate()`—Fired when the object is about to be swapped out of memory.
- `ejbActivate()`—Fired when the object is paged back into memory.
- `ejbRemove()`—Fired when the object is destroyed.
- `setSessionContext()` / `setEntityContext()`—Fired when a reference to the bean context is passed to the bean. You can use this method to cache the context reference, which allows your bean to contact the EJB container. This can be very useful if you are using environment properties (described later in this topic).

Entity beans have several additional callbacks that will be discussed in the Entity Bean section:

- `ejbFind<METHOD>()`—A means of searching for and returning a reference to one or more entity beans. <METHOD> can be any set of words that matches a corresponding `find<METHOD>()` on the EJB's home interface.
- `ejbLoad()`—Fires when the container wants the bean to refresh any cached data.
- `ejbStore()`—Fires when the container wants the bean to flush any changed cached data to the database.
- `unsetEntityContext()`—The EJB container will call this method just before releasing the bean for garbage collection.

This method allows the bean to release any reference back to the EntityContext.

Programmatic Services: Contexts and Environment

While much of the runtime environment is transparently managed by the server and the container, you can manipulate specific settings exposed in the `SessionContext` and `EntityContext` objects (available to session beans and entity beans, respectively). The context is also a means to supplement or override container-managed transactions or security checks, and can be used to obtain a reference to the bean's `EJBObject` interceptor. In some circumstances, you will want to pass this reference to another bean so that the second bean can make calls on the first bean.

The most common programmatic services are:

- Fine-grained security—EJBs have programmatic access to security roles for fine-grain authorization checks.
- Transaction abort—Any automatic transaction started by the container can be aborted programmatically. For more on transactions, see the Transactions topic later in the chapter.
- Fine-grained transactions—Session beans can programmatically demarcate their own transaction begin and commit points.
- Resources—Through the EJB environment, an EJB can programmatically reference other remote objects, database connections, message systems, and other external resources.

A more detailed discussion of the EJB environment can be found in the Basic Beans topic later in this chapter.

Deployment Descriptors

The deployment descriptor, a standardized XML file, describes various aspects of the EJB, including its automatic transaction and security settings. Each vendor provides a set of deployment tools that read the EJB deployment descriptor (and often a vendor-specific deployment descriptor that contains extra settings) and generates the interceptor objects and RMI stubs. The deployment descriptor is also the key mechanism for EJB portability across servers.

Topic: Basic Beans

The most basic bean is a stateless session bean. This chapter illustrates many of the concepts used by all bean types through examples based on stateless session beans.

As mentioned previously, a stateless session bean is an object with "fire and forget" methods. The bean does not retain any information between method executions. These beans are generally very fast and very simple. Stateless session beans are used to perform actions in a very small, fast package.

CORE CONCEPTS

Programming Model: One Client at a Time

When a client accesses a session bean, the bean acts as if it is single-threaded. In other words, each client accesses a unique bean instance. The bean cannot be accessed concurrently or by any other client.

Under the covers, most EJB containers actually retain a pool of stateless session beans for ready access. When a client requests a bean, it is taken out of the pool. When the client calls `remove()` on the bean, it is returned to the pool. Stateful session beans and entity beans are handled somewhat differently, as illustrated in later topics.

EJB Environment

The EJB container and J2EE server expose certain environment resources. These resources can include message system connectors, database connectors, sockets, EJBs, security role references, and key-value data pairs. You can think of the EJB environment as a JNDI-enabled configuration file that your EJBs can use to configure themselves. You define the resources and environment settings at deployment in an XML deployment descriptor file rather than in code.

To illustrate the utility of environment resources, consider an EJB that connects to a database through a `javax.sql.DataSource` object, explained in the Drivers and Connections topic of Chapter 3. The EJB must initialize the correct JDBC driver and generate a `DataSource`. However, this limits the EJB's portability, because the programmer is required to know the JDBC driver and database URL at compile time. If the driver or URL changes, the EJB has to be modified and recompiled. Environment resources provide a way around this by providing a JNDI-accessible naming service with resource bindings. The EJB can simply ask the environment for a reference to the `DataSource`. The

DataSource object will be created and initialized by the application server.

A resource factory reference is a piece of the deployment descriptor that describes the resources available to an EJB. The EJB spec outlines a few standard resources supported by all containers:

- A JavaMail session—Used for connecting to an e-mail server (POP3, SMTP, etc.).
- A URL—EJBs can reference URLs such as Servlets and JSPs that are part of the application. Use these factories for connecting to web pages.
- DataSource—The DataSource is a JDBC factory for java.SQL.Connection objects. Use this resource for connecting to relational databases.
- ConnectionFactory—The Java Messaging Service uses javax.jms.ConnectionFactory in a fashion similar to a JavaMail session or JDBC DataSource. JMS is described in a series of CodeNotes web articles CN J2010002.

The EJB environment also exposes data (key/value pairs), references to other EJBs, and additional vendor-specific resource factories.

An EJB programmer must create arbitrary names to expose the references he requires. These reference names are then linked to the actual resources, data elements, and other EJBs through the EJB deployment descriptor. For example, an EJB that needs to connect to a DataSource might use the following code to "look up" the environment resource named "env/jdbc/MyDatasource":

```
/**assumes import of java.sql.*, javax.sql.*, and javax.naming.*
**/
InitialContext ic = new InitialContext();
DataSource ds = (DataSource)
          ic.lookup("java:comp/env/jdbc/MyDatasource");
Connection conn = ds.getConnection();
```

Listing 7.9 Connecting to a DataSource environment resource

This code uses a JNDI InitialContext to reference the environment. The application server exposes the environment through a JNDI naming interface. Several examples of other environment resources are provided in the Examples section of this topic.

Creating Environment Entries

Environment entries are created during deployment by adding specific tags to the deployment descriptor. The environment descriptor settings are explained in detail in Chapter 9. For now, consider a few example tags:

```
<!-- A JDBC Datasource -->
<resource-ref>
  <res-ref-name>jdbc/MyDatasourc</res-ref-name>
  <res-type>javax.sql.DataSource</res-type>
  <res-auth>application</res-auth>
</resource-ref>
<!-- An EJB resource -->
<ejb-ref>
  <ejb-ref-name>ejb/AccountHomeRef</ejb-ref-name>
  <ejb-ref-type>Entity</ejb-ref-type>
  <home>com.codenotes.j2ee.ejb.AccountHome</home>
  <remote>com.codenotes.j2ee.ejb.AccountRemote</remote>
  <ejb-link>Account</ejb-link>
<ejb-ref>
<!-- A String value -->
<env-entry>
  <env-entry-name>ClientName</env-entry-name>
  <env-entry-type>java.lang.String</env-entry-type>
  <env-entry-value>CodeNotes</env-entry-value>
</env-entry>
```

Listing 7.10 Some example environment deployment descriptor tags

With the above deployment descriptor, an EJB could use JNDI to "look up" and obtain a reference for a `javax.sql.Datasource` (as illustrated in Listing 7.9 above), a connection to an EJB named `AccountHomeRef`, and a `java.lang.String` key-value pair named "ClientName" with a value of "CodeNotes."

Data Access Pattern

Both stateless and stateful session beans may need to access databases. Because EJBs are distributed objects rather than fixed clients, it is important to limit database access to quick surgical strikes. An EJB has a highly variable life span and should not maintain a lock on database resources any longer than necessary. The basic database access pattern described in Chapter 3 (JDBC) is even more important with EJBs:

1. Obtain resources—Create the `Connection`, `Statement`, and `ResultSet`.
2. Perform work—Process the `ResultSet` quickly, or convert it to another object type (`List`, `Map`, `Set`, etc.).

3. Release resources—Close your `ResultSet`, `Statement`, and `Connection` as soon as possible.

Dependent Value Classes

To support the data access pattern of quick database access, most EJBs use some sort of Dependent Value Class (DVC). A DVC is a Java class that implements the `java.io.Serializable` interface, denoting that it is passed over the network by value. These classes are network-safe helper classes that store data for an EJB and can be used to transport data from an EJB to a client. Some DVCs already exist in the Java 2 Standard Edition, including primitive object types (`java.lang.String`) and the `java.util.Collection` classes (`List, Set, Map`).

Another advantage of a DVC is that you can use it to implement specific data validation and support functions. Consider Figure 7.5:

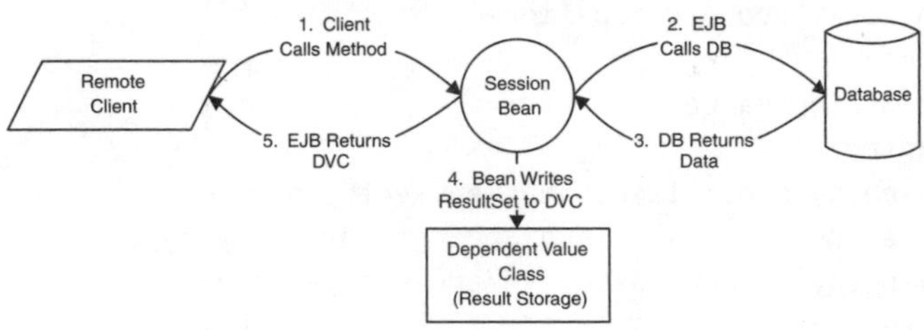

Figure 7.5 Dependent Value Class illustration

The client executes a method on the EJB (Step 1), which performs an SQL call (Step 2). The EJB converts the `ResultSet` (Step 3), to a Dependent Value Class (Step 4), closes all resources, and returns the DVC to the client (Step 5). The client is never directly connected to the database, and the EJB accesses the database just long enough to create and fill the DVC.

Stateless session beans will not maintain references to DVCs after their initial use. In other words, once the original client-to-EJB method call is finished, the EJB "forgets" about its copy of the Dependent Value Class, and the DVC will be garbage-collected on the server. With Stateful session beans, Dependent Value Classes can be stored for later reuse.

EXAMPLE

The example at the beginning of the chapter is a well-documented stateless session bean. The following examples are code fragments for use inside all types of beans.

Accessing Environment Settings

Note that all of the following code fragments use the jndi.properties file provided by the application server to set the `InitialContext`. If you need a refresher on `InitialContext` or the jndi.properties file, you may wish to refer to the JNDI topic in Chapter 4.

```
//Key-Value Pair example
String clientName = (String)ic.lookup("java:comp/env/ClientName");
System.out.println(clientName + "'s E-commerce Center");
//E-mail Session example
//assumes import of javax.mail.*, javax.mail.internet.*
Session mailSession = (Session) new InitialContext().lookup(
  "java:comp/env/mail/MailSession");
InternetAddress address = new
   InternetAddress("info@infusiondev.com");
Transport transport = mailSession.getTransport(address);
//EJB Reference Example
//assumes import of javax.ejb
Object homeRef = new InitialContext().lookup(
  "java:comp/env/ejb/AccountHomeRef");
AccountHome home = (AccountHome) PortableRemoteObject.narrow(
  homeRef, com.codenotes.j2ee.ejb.AccountHome.class);
Account anAccount = home.create();
```

Listing 7.11 Environment settings examples

HOW AND WHY

Why Do I Use Stateless Session Beans?

With stateless session beans, the server can keep track of the request load and pool a smaller number of bean instances, allocating them as needed. Since each object is effectively the same (it has no conversational state), the client cannot tell if a new bean has been created. This transparent pooling saves server resources (CPU time to create new objects and memory to house them). In other words, stateless session beans are a key component of any system that must scale to a large number of users.

Why Do I Downcast EJB Environment References with narrow() and Other Resources Without narrow()?

EJBs are RMI objects handled using the RMI-IIOP protocol. This protocol requires an explicit conversion from the object reference (IOR) to the object class. See the RMI-IIOP concept in Chapter 4 for more details. Resource managers and environment objects, on the other hand, are generally local to the server and are not exposed through RMI-IIOP.

How Do I Store State Persistently in a Stateless Session Bean?

While this question sounds like it doesn't make sense, think of it in this context: You want to take advantage of the speed, clusterability, and features of a stateless session bean but need to store state data that you will retrieve later.

If you want to add state to a stateless session bean, you should use an external data store such as a relational database or persistent cache. Your beans may run a little bit slower because of the additional data access requirements, but you can store state without resorting to entity beans or the overhead of stateful session beans.

BUGS AND CAVEATS

Callbacks and JDBC

The `ejbCreate()` and `ejbRemove()` callbacks are not called within a transactional context in any session bean. If you put database operations in these methods and an error occurs, the database action will not be recovered. This is by design. These methods are specifically meant for bean life cycle control. Because these methods are managed by the EJB container, transactional context is normally irrelevant and is therefore not provided for these specific methods.

Environment Services

If your J2EE server does not provide a particular service through the built-in JNDI service, then you must use JNDI to connect to the external resource. In these cases, you have to explicitly set the JNDI initial context; you can't take advantage of the built-in server environment jndi.properties file or deployment descriptors. For example, if you wanted to use the File SPI to look up the contents of "MyDirectory" and the application server does not support the File SPI, you would have to explicitly set the JNDI `InitialContext`:

```
//assumes import of javax.naming
  java.util.Hashtable env = new java.util.Hashtable();
  env.put(Context.INITIAL_CONTEXT_FACTORY,
    "com.sun.jndi.fscontext.RefFSContextFactory");
  try {
```

```
    Context ctx = new InitialContext(env);
    NamingEnumeration list = ctx.list("MyDirectory");
  ...
```

Listing 7.12 Using an external service

DESIGN NOTES

Fine-Grained vs. Coarse-Grained Access Methods

A bean that potentially exposes a lot of data to a client should map that data to a dependent value class. This can't be overemphasized. Fewer large network operations are almost always faster than smaller, more frequent operations. Network latency (overhead) always degrades the speed of smaller operations when you add them up. By encapsulating data into a single serializable class object, you reduce the network traffic significantly.

Object/Relational Mapping

Synchronizing an object model with a relational database is known as object/relational (O/R) mapping. The task isn't necessarily hard, but it is tedious to write, and especially tedious to optimize. See the CodeNotes website for more information about O/R tools CN J2070001.

Move the InitialContext to a Cache

If you have a lot of environment settings, it might be beneficial to cache your `InitialContext`. By caching the `InitialContext`, you can save the overhead of creating a new one for each resource you want to access. The process for caching the `InitialContext` is:

1. Create an instance variable for the `InitialContext` in your EJB.
2. Load your `InitialContext` into the instance variable on your `ejbActivate()` and `ejbCreate()` methods. These methods start the bean life cycle.
3. Set your `InitialContext` reference to null on the `ejbPassivate()` and `ejbRemove()` methods. This will free up resources when the bean is passivated or dies.

SUMMARY

Stateless session beans are the simplest beans to write and use. Many of the concepts discussed are relevant to all bean types. In particular, you should note that:

- All EJBs can access environment settings.
- Database operations should be short and quick.
- Stateless session beans are used for "fire and forget" business methods and do not retain state.

These main concepts will be expanded upon in the following topics.

Topic: Stateful Session Beans

With stateless session beans, methods must be short and self-contained, because the bean does not retain memory between calls. Stateful session beans, on the other hand, provide conversational services. The commands issued to these beans are built on the context established by the preceding commands. For complex topics, this type of conversation is usually preferable to a long sequence of simple commands.

Where a stateless session bean is simply a container for direct commands, a stateful session bean can be considered a "conversational agent." The stateful bean retains memory and can perform complex tasks by issuing simple commands to other components.

CORE CONCEPTS

Life Cycle

In order to design efficient stateful session beans, you must know something about how these beans are created, stored, and used. The actual life cycle is defined by the EJB container, access patterns, and your client program.

When you request a new instance of a session bean, the container intercepts the request and executes the `ejbCreate()` command to the EJB (state 1). The EJB stays in active memory until your client explicitly releases it (transition from 1 to 4) or until the container determines that the bean is "inactive." Generally, the container declares a bean inactive if the bean hasn't received a command for a configurable time interval.

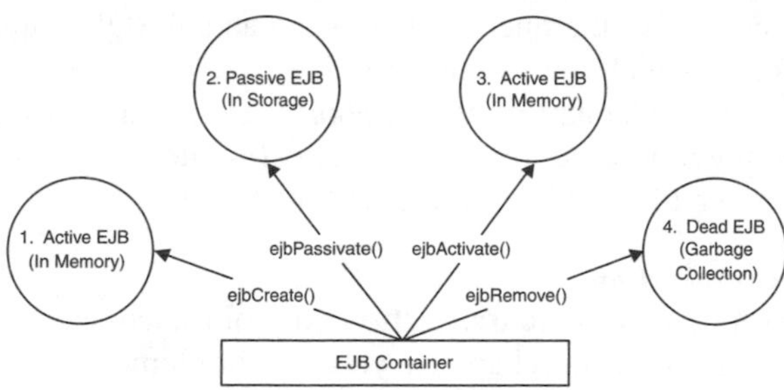

Figure 7.6 Stateful session bean life cycle

The container will execute the `ejbPassivate()` command on the inactive EJB and move it from active memory to storage (transition from 1 to 2). If your client issues a new command to the bean, the container will execute the `ejbActivate()` method to "wake up" the bean before submitting your new command (transition from 2 to 3). Finally, if the EJB stays in storage for a configurable time limit, the container will execute the `ejbRemove()` command to destroy the bean (transition from 2 to 4).

Passivation

A stateful session bean can store data in any format while it is in active memory, but only certain data types can be saved when the bean is passivated. In particular, any member variable that implements the `java.io.Serializable` interface will be saved. This includes Java primitives (`String`, `Float`, etc.), references to other EJBs, Dependent Value Classes, `SessionContext` objects, and environment settings. Provided you use these object types, the entire data content (object graph) of your bean will be saved when the bean is passivated. You can even nest layers. For example, a particular member variable might be a `Serializable` helper class that contains references to other EJBs.

Object types that cannot be saved should be freed on `ejbPassivate()` and brought back on `ejbActivate()`. Resources such as `javax.sql.DataSource` and `javax.mail.Session` are usually handled this way.

For example, consider a stateful session bean that holds the results of an SQL query. The bean would need access to `Connection`, `Statement`, and `ResultSet` objects while it is active. However, none of these objects can or should be stored when the bean is passive, both because they require limited resources (both database and memory) and because the underlying data might change while the bean is passive. The bean should release these objects in `ejbPassivate()` and store the information needed to reestablish the query (such as the actual SQL statement, and an indication of which rows to return).

By properly implementing the `ejbPassivate()` and `ejbActivate()` methods, you will release limited resources (memory, database connections, etc.) and build a much more efficient system.

SessionSynchronization

While EJBs have automatic transaction control (discussed in the Transactions topic later in the chapter), you can implement the `javax.ejb.SessionSynchronization` interface to access an extended set of transaction callbacks. These callbacks are only available in stateful session beans and provide notification when a transaction starts and commits. When you implement this interface, you must define three methods:

- `afterBegin()`—This method is called by the container immediately after the bean is included in a transaction. Generally, you would use this method to establish resources such as database `Connection` and `Statement` objects.
- `beforeCompletion()`—This method is fired immediately before the container attempts to commit the transaction. Use this method to perform any last-minute checks on the resource or data.
- `afterCompletion(boolean committed)`—This method is fired immediately after the transaction is committed. The `boolean` value is `true` if the transaction was committed and `false` if a rollback occurred. Use this method to release system resources and "clean up the mess."

Several examples of `SessionSynchronization` can be found on the CodeNotes website CN J2070002.

EXAMPLE

The following example illustrates a ShoppingCartBean. Note that the `EJBHome` and `EJBObject` interfaces are not shown.

```
package com.codenotes.j2ee.ejb;
import javax.ejb.*;
import java.util.*;
import javax.rmi.PortableRemoteObject;
import javax.naming.*;
public class ShoppingCartBean implements SessionBean {
  SessionContext ctx;
```

```
  List cart;
  UserInformation userInfo;
  public void ejbCreate(UserInformation userInfo) {
    cart = new ArrayList();
    this.userInfo = userInfo;
  }
  public void ejbRemove() {
    ctx = null;
  }
  public void addToCart(ShoppingItem anItem) {
    cart.add(anItem);
  }
  public void removeFromCart(ShoppingItem anItem) {
    cart.remove(anItem);
  }
  public SummaryCharges checkout() {
    Order anOrder = getOrderHome().create(userInfo);
    anOrder.addItems(cart);
    return anOrder.getSummaryCharges();
  }
  public void ejbPassivate() { }
  public void ejbActivate() { }
  public void setSessionContext(SessionContext ctx) {
    this.ctx = ctx;
  }
  private OrderHome getOrderHome() {
    try {
      Object home = new InitialContext().lookup(
        "java:comp/env/ejb/Order");
      return (OrderHome)PortableRemoteObject.narrow(home,
        com.codenotes.j2ee.ejb.OrderHome.class);
    }
    catch (Exception e) {
      throw new EJBException (e);
    }
  }
}
```

Listing 7.13 The ShoppingCart stateful session bean example

Notice that we have to declare the `ejbPassivate()` and `ejbActivate()` methods even though these methods perform no actions.

This bean would use a deployment descriptor similar to the following:

```
<!--Note that line breaks are artificial and should be removed--!
<session>
  <ejb-name>ShoppingCart</ejb-name>
  <home>com.codenotes.j2ee.ejb.ShoppingCartHome</home>
  <remote>com.codenotes.j2ee.ejb.ShoppingCart</remote>
  <ejb-class>com.codenotes.j2ee.ejb.ShoppingCartBean</ejb-class>
  <session-type>Stateful</session-type>
  <transaction-type>Container</transaction-type>
  <ejb-ref>
    <ejb-ref-name>ejb/Order</ejb-ref-name>
    <ejb-ref-type>Entity</ejb-ref-type>
    <home>com.codenotes.j2ee.ejb.OrderHome</home>
    <remote>com.codenotes.j2ee.ejb.Order</remote>
  </ejb-ref>
</session>
<assembly-descriptor>
  <container-transaction>
    <method>
      <ejb-name>ShoppingCart</ejb-name>
      <method-name>addToCart</method-name>
    </method>
    <method>
      <ejb-name>ShoppingCart</ejb-name>
      <method-name>removeFromCart</method-name>
    </method>
    <trans-attribute>NotSupported</trans-attribute>
  </container-transaction>
  <container-transaction>
    <method>
      <ejb-name>ShoppingCart</ejb-name>\
      <method-name>checkout</method-name>
    </method>
    <trans-attribute>Required</trans-attribute>
  </container-transaction>
</assembly-descriptor>
```

Listing 7.14 The ShoppingCart deployment descriptor

Note that the <session-type> tags say “Stateful” instead of “Stateless” as in the earlier Calculator example. This change in the deployment descriptor is one of the primary differences between stateless and stateful session beans.

See the CodeNotes website for full source code and example setup instructions ⚬CN J2070003.

HOW AND WHY

Can I Call a Stateless Session Bean from a Stateful Session Bean?

Yes. In fact, this is a very common design pattern. The stateful session bean acts as an agent for the client, executing one or more methods on stateless session beans or entity beans. However, you have to remember to declare all the referenced beans in the deployment descriptor. For example, the deployment descriptor for a stateful session bean that calls EJB A, EJB B, and EJB C must declare all three beans in <ejb-ref> tags. Otherwise, the EJB deployer will not know that all four beans must be grouped together.

Reversing the order (stateless calling stateful) doesn't make much sense, as the "state" of the stateful session bean adds no value to the stateless session bean.

BUGS AND CAVEATS

Caching

Stateful sessions are great tools for productivity and design simplicity, but they can consume lots of memory if you have many clients. If you cache query data (a very common case), be sure you limit the number of rows retrieved at any time or use a common cache object (e.g., an entity bean) to reduce this memory load.

Clusters

Stateful session beans are usually pinned to one machine. It's hard to load balance among machines, since you would need to replicate the data and/or method calls on each server. See the CodeNotes website for more information ⚬CN J2070004.

Recovery

The EJB specification does not mandate that session beans recover state after a crash. In other words, if the server goes down, your stateful session bean will most likely be destroyed. If you need to maintain state in a reliable fashion, save all the values to a database and set a recovery identifier to requery the database if necessary. See the CodeNotes website for more information ⚬CN J2070005.

DESIGN NOTES

Stateful session beans are most often called directly from web applications (Servlets, JSPs, or helper classes for these objects) or application-clients. Stateful session beans act as the primary gateway between the client, the other bean types (stateless session beans and entity beans), and the database. Several common design patterns for using these beans are available on the CodeNotes website CN J2070006.

SUMMARY

Stateful session beans differ from stateless session beans in two significant ways. First, stateful beans retain memory between calls. This provides a conversational context that is absent from stateless beans. Second, stateful beans have access to `SessionSynchronization`, which provides extra callbacks for transactional methods. Transactions are described in detail in the next topic.

Topic: Transactions

Transactions are the units of work that define your system. Any method or function that is part of a transaction must be reversed if any part of the transaction fails. For example, consider a transfer between bank accounts. The transfer involves debiting (withdrawing) an amount from the first account and crediting (adding) the amount to the second account. Unless both debit *and* credit actions can be performed, neither one should be. The "transfer" transaction would contain both the "debit" action and the "credit" action.

Transactions were introduced in the Advanced JDBC topic of Chapter 3 (JDBC). However, JDBC transactions are limited to SQL statements. J2EE provides a framework for transactions that extends outside the database and incorporates actual EJB method calls. Note that unlike other transactional models (COM in particular), EJB transactional control is method-level. Each method on an EJB may be individually configured with a different transaction level.

This section will take you through the possible J2EE transaction settings, composing transactions out of several EJBs, and some common design patterns. If you have never worked with transactions, the CodeNotes website has a refresher article CN J2070007.

CORE CONCEPTS

Call Paths

If you consider that a transaction is a sequence of actions, the sequence may span many different objects. The sequence of actions (fired on the objects) makes up a call path. Call paths can be simple or complex, as illustrated in Figure 7.7.

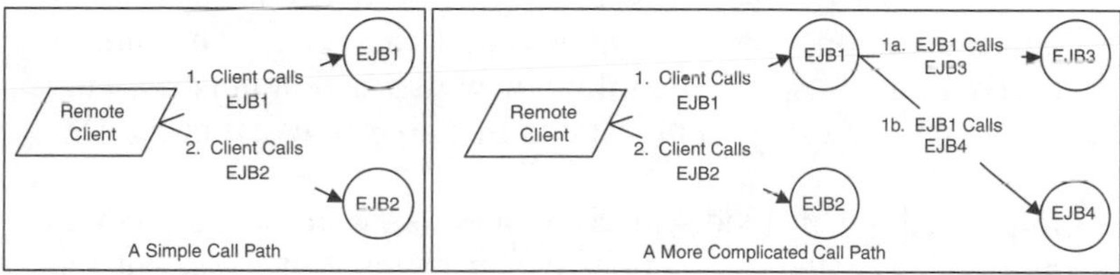

Figure 7.7 Some typical call paths

Any object that is part of a call path can only be used in one transaction at a time. This object locking is critical for the ability to "rollback" or revert the changes caused by a transaction.

Commit and Rollback

If all the methods inside a transaction complete successfully, the transaction is "committed" and the data changes become permanent. However, if any part of a transaction fails, the transaction must rollback.

With JDBC (Chapter 3, Advanced JDBC topic), you have to explicitly tell the `Connection` to commit or rollback changes. With EJBs, the container takes care of these operations for you. As soon as a call path is complete, the container will commit the changes. If any exception occurs and is not caught, the container will automatically perform a rollback.

The CodeNotes website has several detailed examples of how to force rollbacks CN `J2070020`. In general, however, all you have to do is throw an exception that isn't explicitly handled by the calling class, within the transactional context.

Container Managed Transactions

In many cases, the EJB developer doesn't need to know very much about transactions. The J2EE environment takes care of all implementation details. However, the developer must configure each bean method to work with possible transactions. This configuration is built into the deployment descriptor and described in Chapter 8 (Packaging and Deployment). However, the six types of transaction support are very important for all EJBs and are described here.

- Required—If a method is configured with Required, it will either use the existing transaction or start a new one, if its caller is not in a transaction. Either way, this setting indicates that a particular method must always be part of a transaction. This is the most common setting for EJB methods.
- RequiresNew—A method with RequiresNew will always start a new transaction, even if its caller is in a transaction. The current transaction is suspended until the new transaction finishes. This has some interesting ramifications that are discussed in the Design Notes section of this topic.
- Supported—A method with Supported is aware of transactions and will pass the transaction to any methods it calls, but the method does not have to be part of a transaction. The method will not, however, be affected by either a commit or rollback of a transaction.
- NotSupported—Some methods, such as socket access, are inherently incompatible with the notion of transactions. These methods can be configured with NotSupported, which will suspend the current transaction (if there is one) before execution and resume it after execution. Use this setting sparingly and with great care.
- Mandatory—The Mandatory setting will throw `javax.transaction.TransactionRequiredException` if the method is not part of a pre-existing transaction. These methods must be part of a transaction but cannot independently create one.
- Never—The Never setting will throw a `java.rmi.RemoteException` if the method is part of a transaction. This setting is almost never used.

Bean-Managed Transactions

Stateful session beans can use programmatic methods to create transactions, as opposed to the declarative model of transactions described so far. This access requires use of the Java Transaction API and is discussed on the CodeNotes website CN J2070008.

EXAMPLE

The transactional context is set as part of the <assembly-descriptor> section of an EJB deployment descriptor. In the earlier Shopping Cart example (Listing 7.14), the "checkout" method was assigned to Required, meaning that the method must be part of a transaction and will create a new one if necessary:

```
<assembly-descriptor>
  ...
  <container-transaction>
    <method>
      <ejb-name>ShoppingCart</ejb-name>\
      <method-name>checkout</method-name>
    </method>
    <trans-attribute>Required</trans-attribute>
  </container-transaction>
</assembly-descriptor>
```

Listing 7.15 Configuring transaction settings

Unfortunately, transaction examples require too many objects to list the code in this format. See the CodeNotes website for several examples illustrating transactions CN J2070009.

HOW AND WHY

When Do I Use RequiresNew?

When a transaction is very large, you may want to split it into multiple transactions. The only drawback with using `RequiresNew` is that a rollback on the first transaction will not undo the actions of the second. You need to build an "inverse transaction" that is called to clean up the mess. See the CodeNotes website for more details CN J2070010.

Another application for `RequiresNew` is building an audit trail. With most audit trails, the fact that an attempt was made is as important as the fact that an action was completed or failed. You can spin the "Build Audit Trail Entry" functionality into a new transaction, so that it will not be reversed if the main transaction fails.

When Do I Use Never or NotSupported

These settings are used with nontransactional operations such as modifying the fields of a stateful session bean, socket communications, accessing URLs, and other cases where the client should not assume transactional safety.

BUGS AND CAVEATS

Entity Beans

Entity bean methods should not be set to `Never`, `NotSupported`, or `Supports`. These settings conflict with the ability of an entity bean to work with the database through `ejbLoad()` and `ejbStore()` methods.

Contention

Contention occurs when two transactions require the same resource (object or method). The first transaction must finish (commit or rollback) before the second transaction can access the resource. Contention is the classic tragedy of the commons scenario, where services tend to overuse or hug the common shared resources more than they really need to.

Solving contention requires that each call path be analyzed for its resource usage. The call paths should be designed with a surgical strike approach to resources: get in, do your work, and get out (as quickly and neatly as possible).

If you find that your system is slow, examine the call paths for your transactions.

DESIGN NOTES

Remember that EJBs are supposed to be reusable business components. You can link several components together inside a transaction to perform a complicated business method. The power of the EJB transaction model is that this link can occur at deployment rather than during development.

SUMMARY

Transactions are a subtle but very important concept. One of the benefits of the EJB architecture is that you do not have to think about transactions and transactional security during development. These settings are all configured through XML deployment descriptors at deployment.

Topic: Entity Beans and Bean-Managed Persistence

Entity beans are remote components with persistent identity. Each and every entity bean instance must have a unique key for identification. These beans usually represent coarse-grained business concepts such as a purchase order. While a session bean might be used to create the order, the actual order contents would be stored in an entity bean. The customer, account manager, purchaser, and distributor would all access the purchase order through the unique entity bean.

Most entity beans operate in close cooperation with dependent value classes (see Stateful Session Beans, above) and relational databases.

CORE CONCEPTS

Contractual Differences from Session Beans

While an entity bean may seem very similar to a stateful session bean, there are some distinct differences in the mechanics:

- Implementation—The entity bean implementation class must extend `EntityBean` instead of `SessionBean`.
- `Create methods`—The `create()` methods are optional in the `EJBHome` interface. If a `create()` method is missing, the EJB container will build a default constructor.
- Finder methods—All entity bean home interfaces must have at least one finder method: `findByPrimaryKey()`. Additional finder methods can be built to provide lookup access to specific entity bean instances.
- `ejbCreate()`—The `ejbCreate()` methods inside your implementation must return the primary key class. Note that the `create()` methods on the home interface still return the `EJBObject` interface. Primary keys are discussed in the next section.
- `ejbLoad()` and `ejbStore()`—These methods are used to synchronize cached state with a database.
- EntityContext—Instead of `setSessionContext()` (described in the Basic Beans topic), entity beans use `setEntityContext()` and `unsetEntityContext()`. The unset method removes the active reference to the `EntityContext`, freeing the bean for garbage collection.

Primary Keys

Entity beans need a serializable primary key. The primary key is a unique identifier for each and every instance of the bean. Consider, for example, a purchase order bean. Each instance of the bean is tagged with a unique identification number. When you want to access a particular purchase order (PO), you would access the bean that has a primary key matching the PO number.

An entity bean's primary key *does not necessarily* map directly to a primary key in a database table. An entity bean can be an "aggregate" of several rows and tables joined in a database. With regard to the purchase order, the database table might use an integer value for the primary key while the bean uses the PO number (which might be a `String`).

A primary key can be a Java primitive object wrapper (`java.lang.Integer`, `java.lang.String`, etc.) or a custom object. Custom objects are generally used if the primary key requires compound data. For example, the purchase order might be uniquely identified by the combination of the requesting company ID and the PO number. The primary key would be a custom object combining the two values.

When you create a custom class for a primary key, you must implement `java.io.Serializable` and override the `equals()` and `hashCode()` methods to ensure comparison by value. For example, consider the Purchase Order bean that is identified by the PO number and company ID:

```
public class PurchaseOrderKey implements java.io.Serializable {
  String companyId;
  String orderId;
  public PurcahseOrderKey(String companyId, String orderId) {
    this.companyId = companyId;
    this.orderId = orderId;
  } //constructor
  public boolean equals(Object o) {
    AccountKey key = (AccountKey) o;
    if ((key.companyId.equals(this.companyId)) &&
        (key.orderId.equals(this.orderId))) {return true;}
    else {return false;}
  } //equals
  public int hashCode() {
    // Perform an XOR on the two fields' hash-codes
    // to return a repeatable value.
    return companyId.hashCode() ^ orderId.hashCode();
  } //hashCode
} //class
```

Listing 7.16 A custom PrimaryKey object

FINDER METHODS

Entity beans, unlike session beans, have a specific unique identity. Each instance is uniquely named with a primary key. Therefore, for a particular entity bean to be accessed, the bean must have finder methods. A finder method must be defined in both the `EJBHome` interface and the EJB implementation object.

As mentioned previously, every entity bean home interface must declare the method:

```
EJBObject findByPrimaryKey(PrimaryKeyClass key)
```

and the bean class must implement:

```
PrimaryKeyClass ejbFindByPrimaryKey(PrimaryKeyClass key)
```

More often than not, this is the only finder method necessary for an entity bean. Notice how the `find()` method returns the `EJBObject` interface of the particular bean, but the `ejbFind()` method returns the primary key class. The EJB container is responsible for matching the primary key returned from `ejbFind()` to an `EJBObject` instance, and returning the `EJBObject` instance to the client. A similar process occurs for `create()` methods.

There are actually two kinds of finder methods that are differentiated by the number of returned objects:

- Single object finders—A single object finder returns a specific `EJBObject` instance.
- Multiobject finders—A multiobject finder returns a `java.util.Enumeration` or `java.util.Collection` containing references to several `EJBObject` instances.

For example, consider the purchase order discussed earlier. The `PurchaseOrderBean` might have a single object finder in the form of `findByPrimaryKey()`. If the primary key class is passed in, a single specific instance will be returned. The bean might also have a multiobject finder in the form of `findByCompanyId()`, which would return a `Collection` of all purchase orders open for the company. Note that each EJB reference taken out of a multiobject finder must be downcast using `PortableRemoteObject.narrow()`. Both single object and multiobject finder methods are illustrated in the example for this topic.

LOAD AND STORE METHODS

With Bean-Managed Persistence, the entity bean is responsible for performing all database operations. The bean should preload any frequently used data inside the `ejbLoad()` method and store any changed data inside the `ejbStore()` method. The `ejbLoad()` callback is fired when the entity bean is created or activated, and the `ejbStore()` method is fired when the entity bean is destroyed or passivated.

The EJB specification does not require that you perform all of your database operations inside `ejbLoad()` and `ejbStore()`. In fact, many designs call for a business method that loads or stores specific data. The load and store callbacks are simply provided as notifications of "pending trauma": a transaction is beginning or committing, or an object is being passivated or activated, where `ejbActivate()` or `ejbPassivate()` would be called after the call to `ejbLoad()` or `ejbStore()`. In each of these cases, the bean must synchronize with a database to ensure data integrity.

EXAMPLE

The CodeNotes website contains a complete example of an entity bean that represents a bank account CN `J2070011`. Unfortunately, the complete example is too long for this format. The particularly important fragments are described below.

Data Operations

For this example, we encapsulate our JDBC operations into specific classes for each SQL statement. These classes implement a `DatabaseOperation` interface that can be passed into a `DatabaseOperationsProcessor` class that will contain a standard data access pattern (try/catch/finally, as discussed in the JDBC chapter).

The EJB can pass any required parameters for the query in the `DatabaseOperation` constructor, and then extract any resulting data through custom `get()` methods.

Finder Methods

The account bean has two finder methods. The first method is the mandatory `findByPrimaryKey()` method, and the second returns a collection of references to `AccountBeans` associated with a particular bank branch:

```
public String ejbFindByPrimaryKey(String key)
    throws FinderException {
  FindAccountPrimaryKey findKey = new FindAccountPrimaryKey(key);
  DatabaseOperationProcessor.execute(getDataSource(), findKey);
  if (findKey.keyExists()) return key;
  throw new ObjectNotFoundException();
}

public Collection ejbFindAcccountsByBranch(String branchId) {
  FindAccountsByBranchQuery query =
    new FindAccountsByBranchQuery(branchId);
  DatabaseOperationProcessor.execute(getDataSource(), query);
  return query.getKeys();
}
```

Listing 7.17 Finder methods for AccountBean implementation class

The `AccountHome` interface would have corresponding find methods without the "ejb" prefix.

These finder methods would be used by a client to create an instance of the `AccountBean`. First, the client would create an instance of the `AccountHome`, and then use either finder method to return the actual `AccountBean` (or beans).

```
//Use FindByPrimaryKey
Object homeRef = anInitialContext.lookup("MyAccountHome");
AccountHome accountHome = (AccountHome)
  PortableRemoteObject.narrow(homeRef,
  com.codenotes.j2ee.ejb.AccountHome.class);
Account anAccount = (Account) PortableRemoteObject.narrow(
  accountHome.findByPrimaryKey("A23A3321A"),
  com.codenotes.j2ee.ejb.Account.class);
System.out.println("Account number: " + info.getAccountId() +
  " Name: " + info.getCustomerName() + " Zip: " + info.getZip() );
//Use FindByBranchId
Object homeRef = anInitialContext.lookup("MyAccountHome");
AccountHome accountHome = (AccountHome)
  PortableRemoteObject.narrow(homeRef,
  com.codenotes.j2ee.ejb.AccountHome.class);
Collection accounts = accountHome.findByBranchId("393010393");
Iterator accountsIterator = accounts.iterator();
while (it.hasNext()) {
```

```
  Account anAccount = (Account)
    PortableRemoteObject.narrow( it.next(),
    com.codenotes.j2ee.ejb.Account.class);
  CustomerInformation info = anAccount.getCustomerInformation();
  System.out.println("Account number: " + info.getAccountId()
    + " Name: " + info.getCustomerName() + " Zip: "
    + info.getZip() );
}
```

Listing 7.18 The client uses the finder methods

Note that in the `FindByBranchId()` example, the client must explicitly narrow the `Account` reference using `PortableRemoteObject.narrow()`. Both single object and multiobject finders return the reference to an entity bean, rather than the actual bean instance.

Life Cycle Methods

The other particularly interesting entity bean methods involve the `AccountBean` life cycle. These methods use helper objects (not shown) to launch stored procedures in a database.

```
//Create a New Account
public String ejbCreate(Customer customer, String branchId) {
  this.balance = 0.0;
  this.customer = customer;
  this.branchId = branchId;
  InsertAccountAndCustomer insert =
  new InsertAccountAndCustomer(branchId, balance, customer);
  DatabaseOperationProcessor.execute(getDataSource(), insert);
  this.accountId = insert.getAccountId();
  return accountId;
}
/** ejbPostCreate is used to allow two-phase creation, necessary
when you use a primary key created by the database */
public void ejbPostCreate() {}
//Remove an Account
public void ejbRemove() {
  DeleteAccountAndCustomer account = new
    DeleteAccountAndCustomer(accountId);
  DatabaseOperationProcessor.execute(getDataSource(), account);
}
//Retrieve an account from the database
public void ejbLoad() {
```

```
  balanceChanged = false;
  customerChanged = false;
  accountId = (String) ctx.getPrimaryKey();
  LoadAccountData loader = new LoadAccountData(accountId);
  DatabaseOperationProcessor.execute(getDataSource(), loader);
  if loader.noSuchObject())throw new
    NoSuchEntityException ("No such entity: " + accountID);
  this.balance = loader.getBalance();
  this.customer = loader.getCustomer();
  this.branchId = loader.getBranchId();
}
//Update the account in the database
public void ejbStore() {
  if (balanceChanged) {
    UpdateBalance updateBal = new
      UpdateBalance(accountId, balance);
    DatabaseOperationProcessor.execute(getDataSource(), updateBal);
  }
  if (customerChanged) {
    UpdateCustomer updateCustomer = new
       UpdateCustomer(accountId, customer);
    DatabaseOperationProcessor.execute(getDataSource(),
       updateCustomer);
  }
}
```

Listing 7.19 Life cycle methods

Note that `ejbStore()` only performs updates if the data has changed. The `ejbLoad()` methods initially sets the `balancedChanged` and `customerChanged` flags to "false"; the actual business methods (not shown) will toggle the flags to "true" if the data is modified.

HOW AND WHY

How Do I Generate Primary Keys, or Use a Database's Primary Key Generator (Oracle Sequences, Sybase Identity Columns, SQL Server Autonumbers, etc.)?

Unfortunately, no uniform method currently exists for accessing an automatically generated key value. Generally, a stored procedure is required, or a universally unique identifier service should be used. The CodeNotes website has several examples of these methods CN J2070012.

Because JDBC 3.0 standardizes getting an "autonumber" value back from an INSERT statement, this feature may be accessible as part of the upcoming J2SE 1.4 and J2EE 1.3 releases.

If you are using "autonumber" generation, you may need to use the `ejbPostCreate()` method to retrieve the new ID from the database after you have inserted the data with `ejbCreate()`.

BUGS AND CAVEATS

Finder Methods and Performance

Each object returned by a finder method is a reference to an EJB that potentially requires a remote method call, implying that all parameters are copied using Java serialization. Each time one of these references is used, at least one more network request is made (to access the object instead of the reference). The performance penalty of these extra trips can be intolerable when finding and using a large number of beans.

Some EJB servers have optimizations that short-circuit the remote method call to EJBs if the server can detect that the call is from another EJB in the same virtual machine. Such an optimization is nonstandard and should not be relied on if you want to create portable entity beans. Having said that, this optimization is often crucial if you want to use entity beans in your systems. EJB 2.0 may fix this limitation by introducing local EJB objects (see Chapter 9, Darkside).

Finder Methods and Database Performance

Multiobject finders in a Bean-Managed Persistence (BMP) bean should return a small number of beans (five to ten) at a time if the returned beans load data with `ejbLoad()`. A finder method BMP implementation only returns primary keys to the container. To actually use the bean, the container makes database calls to load the data. Such transactions usually require a minimum of N+1 database queries, where N is the number of primary keys returned in your finder method. Sometimes the beans can be cached in memory, justifying the penalty. However, there are restrictions on caching (see below). In general, performing this many database calls is hard to justify, almost completely eliminating the utility of multiobject finder methods when using BMP.

If you really want to use multiobject finder methods, the first solution is to use Container-Managed Persistence (CMP). In CMP (described in the next topic), finder methods can be optimized for higher performance.

A somewhat controversial workaround to this finder performance problem involves "Fat Primary Keys," which encapsulate all bean data. See the CodeNotes website for a discussion and example of this pattern CN J2070013.

Caching and Concurrency

Generally, entity beans can be cached on the server if and only if the EJB server owns the database schema. In other words, no other systems can make updates. This requirement stems from the difficulty in propagating database updates back to the EJB server and still maintaining data integrity.

Servers that cache beans in this way have a pessimistic concurrency policy, where the EJB server itself will lock all concurrent access to entity beans. This policy is often unacceptable if you have large beans with a significant number of read-only attributes, or you have a large number of clients that read from a bean and only a small number that write to the bean. By default, the EJB server will not differentiate between readers and writers. All clients will be exclusively locked out from concurrent access. BMP entity beans generally are not suitable for a cache. CMP entity beans can be, as some servers provide a scalable implementation of fine-grained entity beans, or even object-locking with a proprietary API.

The most common policy is to rely on the underlying database for locking. This concurrency policy provides a much finer-grained locking approach and is recommended. Multiple concurrent operations can occur on an entity bean, as the server will merely create replicas or clones of the EJB for each concurrent transaction and let the database sort out the conflicts.

Most servers have settings to tweak their locking policy (also known as their commit option). See the CodeNotes website for server-specific examples and a more detailed explanation CN J2070014.

DESIGN NOTES

Entity Bean Design Patterns

A BMP bean should represent an aggregate entity that covers a range of data in the database (multiple rows or multiple tables), not just a single row. This way, the bean can provide its own finderlike methods on the `EJBObject` interface, using regular queries mapped to dependent value classes. See the CodeNotes website for several examples CN J2070015.

Change Tracking

Keep track of your cached changes. If you have lots of little objects, use a "dirty flag" to mark changes on each object. By only updating "dirty" objects, you can save significant overhead. Some EJB servers have proprietary hooks to a particular "dirty method" name on the EJB itself, to know if a call to the `ejbStore()` method should occur at all.

SUMMARY

Unlike session beans, entity beans have a unique identity. These beans are particularly well suited to back-end database access. Generally, these beans are exposed to clients indirectly through methods on session beans.

When you develop an entity bean with Bean-Managed Persistence, you are responsible for generating all of the database access code. As you can see from the example in this section, this code is basic but voluminous. The next topic covers entity beans with Container-Managed Persistence. These beans take advantage of the container to perform object-relational mapping and generation of database access methods.

Topic: Container-Managed Persistence

One of the major aims of entity beans is to explore the idea that software components can be independent of the underlying database. By decoupling the object code from the database, business objects can be developed much faster in a more flexible way. The database can be optimized for specific needs and then mapped to standard code components during deployment.

Deployment tools can help specify the mapping between an EJB and the underlying database, which can be an object database, legacy data store (mainframe), or relational database. The tools can then generate code to perform data operations or can leverage a runtime framework to dynamically generate SQL. Several mapping products (e.g., TopLink) have been available for some time but have not had the support of a complete code framework such as J2EE.

Container-Managed Persistence (CMP) entity beans are specifically designed to provide a framework for this model. As such, CMP beans are tied much closer to both the database and the specific EJB container than Bean-Managed Persistence entity beans and session beans.

While the concepts behind CMP entity beans are not that difficult, a successful deployment of CMPs is highly dependent on the quality of the EJB container, and your experience with the various deployment tools (which are usually expensive!). In other words, working with CMPs is not something you want to try on your first J2EE architecture.

CORE CONCEPTS

Primary Keys Revisited

CMP entity bean custom primary keys differ from BMP custom primary keys in several ways:

- Field mapping—The underlying fields of a custom primary key must be mapped to one or more database fields. If the primary key is then mapped to a single field in the CMP entity bean, the primary key field must be a `Serializable` object (i.e., instead of using `int`, use `java.lang.Integer`).
- Custom keys—Custom keys (compound keys) are based on more than one field in the EJB. The primary key fields in both the primary key class and the EJB class should be identically named and declared `public`.
- Create methods—Since a container has the freedom to generate primary keys for the user, all `ejbCreate()` methods must return `null` instead of the primary key value.

The EJB container will automatically populate the primary key fields from the EJB class. As can be seen in the next section, these changes in primary keys allow the container to perform complex actions regarding relationships.

Create and Find Methods

A CMP entity bean is not required to implement `ejbFind()` methods to match the `find()` methods in the remote interface. Instead, the EJB container will provide an implementation of these methods, based on proprietary configuration tools or vendor-specific deployment descriptors. Often, a vendor will define a SQL-like object query language to define the finder methods.

EJB 2.0 standardizes this approach with EJB QL (see Chapter 9, Darkside).

The Container and CMP Fields

With regard to CMP entity beans, the EJB container does much more than provide an interface to the server. The container is also responsible for generating and performing SQL queries against the database for loading and saving bean data. With BMP entity beans, the developer is responsible for these tasks.

The basic CMP EJB deployment descriptor identifies each field in the entity bean. The vendor-specific deployment descriptor actually maps these fields to the database tables and fields. Several vendor deployment descriptor examples are available on the CodeNotes website CN J2070016.

The EJB descriptor must expose every persistent field in the CMP entity bean. A typical tag might look like:

```
<cmp-field>
  <field-name>orderId</field-name>
</cmp-field>
<cmp-field>
  <field-name>orderType</field-name>
</cmp-field>
<cmp-field>
  <field-name>myCustomer</field-name>
</cmp-field>
```

Listing 7.20 A <cmp-field> tag

The container will match these fields to the vendor-specific descriptor and load the data into the bean. This process is very intuitive for normal fields such as "orderId" and "orderType."

However, the process changes for foreign keys that relate to other CMP entity beans, such as "myCustomer." If a field represents another EJB, the container will use the field value as the primary key to generate a new instance of the second EJB. This is actually the support method for one-to-one relationships. When you instantiate Bean A, you automatically get an instance of Bean B (provided that Bean B's primary key is fully identified in the deployment descriptor of Bean A).

The process for creating related EJBs follows several steps, illustrated below with the `OrderBean` and `CustomerBean` example.

1. The Client requests a specific `OrderBean` using the `findByPrimaryKey()` method on the `OrderHome`.
2. The container intercepts the request and creates a new `OrderBean` instance with the specified primary key.

3. The container reads the deployment descriptor and maps the identified database fields to the `OrderBean` fields.
4. When the container encounters the "customerId" field, which maps to a `CustomerBean` object inside the `OrderBean`, the container will automatically generate a new instance of `CustomerBean` and assign the primary key value mapped to the customerId attribute in the `OrderBean`.
5. The container will then automatically load all of the `CustomerBean`'s data and place the `CustomerBean` instance inside the `OrderBean` myCustomer field.

Unfortunately, the EJB 1.1 specification does not provide as nice a feature for complex relationships such as one-to-many or many-to-many.

Complex Relationships

One of the most important aspects of entity beans is modeling object relationships such as one-to-one, one-to-many, and many-to-many. Unfortunately, relationships between CMP EJBs (beyond one-to-one) are not defined by the specification. In other words, each container vendor is free to create a different model for these relationships.

Truly portable CMP entity beans require virtual complex relationships based on using finder methods on other EJB home interfaces. These finder methods search out one-to-many relationships based on the back-reference (i.e., foreign key) to the source object. This pattern is illustrated in Figure 7.8:

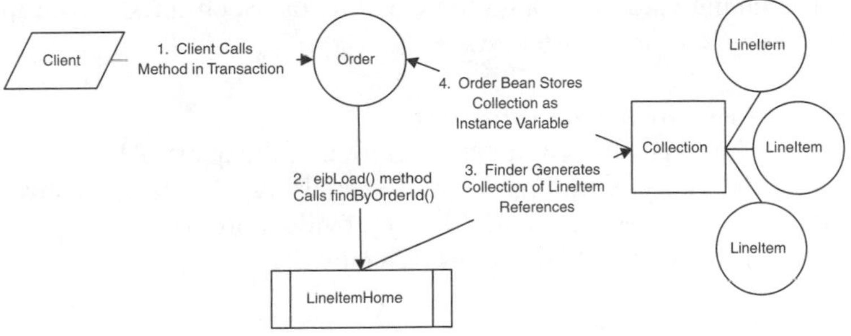

Figure 7.8 One-to-many relationships

As you can see, the one-to-many relationship requires extra code inside the `ejbLoad()` method to generate the collection of references to the `LineItems` associated with the `Order`. This collection provides the equivalent of what is ordinarily a simple SQL statement (e.g., SELECT * from lineitems where orderid = X).

The EJB 2.0 specification currently includes standardized support for these types of complex relationships.

EXAMPLE

The CodeNotes website has the complete code for an example based on Figure 7.8 CN J2070017. This example uses the J2EE reference implementation and leverages one-to-one and one-to-many relationships. Another example of the relationship patterns, using WebGain's TopLink, is also available on the CodeNotes website CN J2070018.

HOW AND WHY

How Do I Optimize Database Retrieval?

Unfortunately, query optimization depends heavily on the particular EJB container and J2EE server. Sophisticated implementations allow for batch loading of relationships and joins, which can dramatically improve performance. Basic implementations (such as the J2EE reference implementation) do not provide any support for optimization.

Can I Use JDBC Calls in a CMP Bean?

Yes, you can use JDBC just like in a regular session bean or BMP entity bean. Just be sure these calls don't interfere with the data that the container is taking care of through the CMP fields. Such interference may result in database inconsistency.

How Do I Generate Dynamic Queries?

Finder methods usually require predefinition of the query. At times, constructing the query at runtime is an essential task. Some sophisticated CMP tools (e.g., WebGain's TopLink) provide a proprietary query API that can compose SQL-like queries dynamically.

BUGS AND CAVEATS

Basic Implementations

Many popular EJB servers have opted to implement CMP in a fashion similar to the J2EE reference implementation; that is, the server meets the bare minimum specification requirements. This unfortunate reality has led to the stigma that a severe performance penalty is associated with CMP, since database operations cannot be properly optimized.

The concept behind CMP is sound, however, and it has the potential to be faster than hand-coded JDBC calls. A successful deployment simply requires a more sophisticated EJB server.

Remote Relationships

Since all EJBs are RMI objects, one may be tempted to create one-to-one and one-to-many CMP entity bean relationships between different physical servers. Such an approach has severe performance penalties, since all calls must be serialized over the network and there is little or no chance that any database optimizations can be performed by the EJB container.

It is recommended that related CMP entity beans be co-located on the same server unless the CMP implementation has explicit support for a clustered environment. WebGain's TopLink, for example, supports a clustered environment on WebLogic and WebSphere.

Learning Curve

While CMP entity beans and their associated tools have tremendous productivity and performance potential, they suffer from being a relatively new approach to modeling enterprise applications. Sophisticated CMP implementations have rich configuration tools and frameworks to supplement the CMP specification, but require significant effort to master the vendor-specific API and tools. Once past the learning curve, productivity gains using object/relational mapping tools have been known to be quite significant.

Also note that some object/relational mapping tools implement a CMP-like framework using regular Java objects and session beans.

DESIGN NOTES

Manipulating Sets of Data

Using CMP entity beans provides a model of data manipulation similar to an object database system. Such systems provide a one-object-at-a-time view of the data, useful for modeling complex constraints and business rules or traversing quickly through a graph of objects. Operations that update large sets of data should use a set-oriented language (such as SQL calls with JDBC). Relational databases are optimized to perform such operations very quickly.

SUMMARY

Container-Managed Persistence works best with tools that go outside the basic EJB specification. Therefore, almost every CMP entity bean deployment is heavily tied to a specific vendor. Use CMP entity beans with extreme caution, unless you are working with one of the advanced tools.

The EJB 2.0 specification (due out late 2001) provides much better support for Container-Managed Persistence. See Chapter 9 (Darkside) for more information about the changes in the EJB 2.0 specification and how they relate to CMP entity beans.

Chapter Summary

Enterprise JavaBeans have received more press and are the subject of more books than any other part of J2EE. The EJB standard is an incredibly rich extension of traditional distributed computing. Unfortunately, the core concepts of EJB are often shrouded in complicated design patterns, hand-waving, and marketing-speak. When you work with EJBs, remember that the mechanics are simple, and there are only a few critical concepts:

- EJBs are basically RMI-IIOP objects. You need an EJBHome interface, an EJBObject interface, and an implementation class.
- Session beans (stateless and stateful) are your primary business tools *and* the main interface between the client and the back-end systems.
- Entity beans (BMP and CMP) are the heart of any J2EE back-end system. These beans have a permanent identity and represent data objects. Entity beans are the primary interface between session beans and any data source such as a relational database.
- The EJB container and J2EE application server are your friends. These programs build code, manage resources, and provide services in a way that is configured during deployment, rather than bean development.

In the next chapter, you will see how the EJBs, along with web applications and application-clients, are rolled into the overall J2EE application framework.

EJB 2.0

At the time of this writing, the EJB 2.0 draft is in final public review. The revised specification contains many new features, including local EJB interfaces. Some of these features are described in Chapter 9 (Darkside). However, you should check the CodeNotes website for additional examples and discussion as the specification is formalized CN J2070019.

Chapter 8

PACKAGING AND DEPLOYMENT

Packaging and deployment are the most important and least understood aspects of J2EE. Although the basic concepts are straightforward, the details and the vendor-specific nature of deployment can cause some serious headaches.

Some J2EE servers (such as Orion—`www.orionserver.com/`) have graphical tools that will lead you through a deployment and will automatically generate some or all of the deployment descriptor files. Other servers (such as BEA WebLogic) have minimal tools or require that you build all of the descriptors and archives yourself. In either case, you need at least a basic understanding of what goes on during a deployment.

This chapter will explain the steps involved in deploying J2EE systems and will provide common scenarios for several application servers.

What Is Involved in Packaging and Deployment?

As indicated in Figure 8.1, a typical J2EE deployment involves one or more components packaged into an enterprise application, which is deployed in a container. The container for a J2EE application is commonly called a J2EE server.

In the following sections, you will find instructions for the three major pieces of a deployment:

- Building archive files for components (EJB JARs, application-client JARs, and WARs) and J2EE applications (EARs).

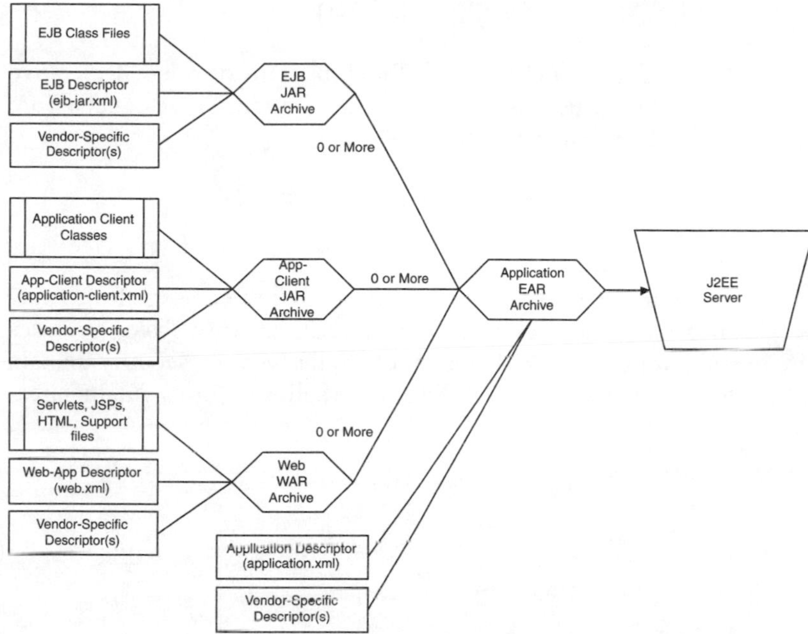

Figure 8.1 An overview of deployment. Components are built into EJB JARs, application-client JARs, and Web WARs. Components are combined into an EAR, which is stored on the J2EE server.

- Creating the deployment descriptors for each component type and the application. Deployment descriptors are XML files that perform several tasks:
  - Describing the component's attributes
  - Providing environment entries and references
  - Defining security levels
- Vendor-specific configuration. Each vendor may use additional deployment descriptors.

One of the critical aspects of deployment is security definition. The J2EE security policy is explained in a separate topic, even though security is configured through the deployment descriptors.

Topic: Security

The J2EE security model can be defined in terms of roles, declarative security, programmatic security, and authentication. These concepts are illustrated in the following sections.

ROLES

A role is simply an abstract container for one or more users. Roles play a critical component in every aspect of J2EE security. Role interfaces are linked through vendor-specific tools to the server's security domain and authentication system. This link is the pathway for user authentication.

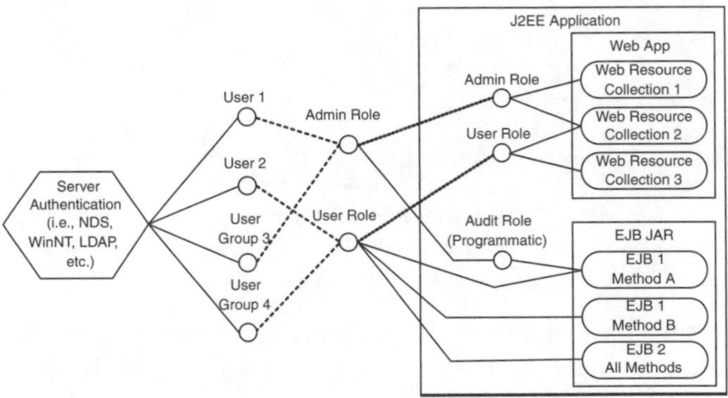

Figure 8.2 Roles are exposed by web applications, EJB JARs, and enterprise archives. The J2EE server (not shown) maps these roles to users and user groups on the server.

Several important concepts are illustrated in Figure 8.2:

- The J2EE server will handle the mapping of local users and user groups to the roles exposed by the application and/or components. In the figure, User 1 and User Group 3 are mapped to the Admin role, while User 2 and User Group 4 are mapped to the User role. If User 1 logs in, he will automatically have access to any object connected to the Admin role.
- Roles can be defined in a web application, an EJB JAR, or a J2EE application. In the figure, the enterprise application exposes "Admin" and "User."
- Any component can use a role defined in a higher-level component. In the figure, EJB 2 is assigned to the "User" role, even

though the role is defined in the application and not in the EJB JAR.

- If an application role is identical to a component role, then the application role masks the component role. In the figure, the Admin role exposed by the web application is automatically associated to the Admin role exposed in the application.
- If a component such as an EJB uses a role programmatically, then the role must be declared in the descriptor but can still be remapped to a declarative role. In the figure, EJB 1, method A uses a role named "Audit" programmatically. This role has been remapped to the Admin role defined in the application.

Defining Roles

Roles are defined the same way in every descriptor, although the exact location for role definition tags is different. The basic role definition tag is:

```
<security-role>
  <description>OptionalDescription</description>
  <role-name>rolename</role-name>
</security-role>
```

Listing 8.1 The <security-role> tag

DECLARATIVE SECURITY

Declarative security is used at deployment time to define the access levels for particular roles. Declarative security can be used on individual methods exposed in an EJB, or on a web collection that is a set of Servlets, JSPs, and HTML pages.

EJB Methods

EJB security is provided at the level of individual methods. A role may have execute rights on one or more methods on a bean. If no security is declared for the bean, every role has access rights.

Web Collections

A web collection is a set of one or more JSPs, Servlets, or HTML pages contained in a web archive. Any number of roles may be assigned access rights to this collection.

Applications

Although roles can be declared in applications, these roles cannot be explicitly assigned to any component. Application-level roles are high-level definitions that may override the component-level definitions, if the names match exactly.

PROGRAMMATIC SECURITY

Two Methods

EJBs, Servlets, and JSPs can provide programmatic security by using either the `HttpServletRequest` or `EJBContext` objects. Both of these objects have a method that will tell you if the current user is in a specific role, and another method that will tell you the user's name.

The EJB methods can be accessed only when you have maintained the EJBContext:

```
//assumes getEJBContext method returns current EJBContext
boolean inRole = getEJBContext().isCallerInRole("gooduser");
String username = getEJBContext().getCallerPrincipal.getName();
```

Listing 8.2 Programmatic security in an EJB

JSPs can access these methods through the `request` implicit object, whereas Servlets can access the methods through the `HttpServletRequest` object passed into the `doGet()` or `doPost()` methods. The following example illustrates the JSP version:

```
<!--Find out if user is in a particular role:-->
<%=request.getUserPrincipal().getName()%>
<%if (request.isUserInRole("gooduser")) {
    out.print(" is in the gooduser role"); }
  else {out.print(" is not in the gooduser role");}
%>
```

Listing 8.3 Programmatic security in a JSP

Why Bother?

In some cases, declarative security is not sufficiently granular. For example, consider the following business scenario:

A company might be divided into four regions: north, east, south, and west. A manager in the north region should be allowed to audit accounts in that region but should not be allowed to touch accounts in any other region.

If we have an account bean that has an `audit()` function, we should use declarative security so that any user with the "Manager" role can execute the method. However, we must use programmatic security to make sure the manager is in the correct region:

```
String accountRegion = getAccountRegion();
if (getEJBContext().isCallerinRole(accountRegion))
{    //perform audit function }
else {//manager can't access the audit method}
```

Listing 8.4   Programmatic security in practice

Exposing the Roles

Every object that uses a role programmatically must expose the role using a <security-role-ref> tag and possibly link the role to a declared role. The syntax for the <security-role-ref> tag is common to every descriptor:

```
<security-role-ref>
  <role-name>NameOfRoleUsedInComponent<role-name>
  <role-link>OptionalNameOfDeclaredRole<role-link>
</security-role-ref>
```

Listing 8.5   The security-role-ref tag

Note that the <role-link> tag is an alias that links the programmatic role to a declared role. During development, the programmer can choose any role names he wants. During deployment, these role names can be overridden to match a different set of roles using the <role-link> tag.

USER AUTHENTICATION

Web Applications

Web applications have four defined authentication types. These types all return some form of credentials to the server. The server will perform an authorization check before allowing access to the web application.

- `BASIC`—Basic authentication is handled through the HTTP 1.1 specification. The client browser launches a login page and returns the user name and password to the server for validation. The login page is specific to the browser. For example, Internet Explorer uses the default Windows login page.

- DIGEST—Digest authentication uses a hash formula to convert the user name and password into unintelligible text before transmission to the server. This type is very rarely used.
- FORM—Form authentication is similar to BASIC, except that you get to define the login screen, which may be an HTML page, JSP, or Servlet. The login page must have an HTML form that has this basic structure:

```
<FORM ID="any" METHOD="post" ACTION="j_security_check">
  <INPUT TYPE="text" NAME="j_username" />
  <INPUT TYPE="password" NAME="j_password" />
</FORM>
```

Listing 8.6 FORM security

You can dress up the form, but make sure that the action is "j_security_check" and that text boxes are named "j_username" and "j_password".

- CLIENT-CERT—The final form of authentication involves receipt of a security certificate from the client. This type of authorization is rarely used, as it requires a certificate stored on every client.

For extra security, you can use BASIC or FORM authentication over HTTPS or SSL, although neither method requires it.

Application-Clients

Until the Java Authentication and Authorization Service is formally part of the J2EE spec (J2EE 1.3), application-clients have no defined authentication methods. However, some J2EE client containers support a security mechanism similar to web applications.

Topic: Archives

The Java Archive, or JAR file, is a core component of Java. JAR files are used for the building of class libraries, the packaging of stand-alone applications, and the consolidation of code. The basic JAR file contains a manifest (packing list) and one or more files. JARs generally contain *.class files, but they may also house support files (i.e., pictures, config files, etc.). JAR files are compressed using the standard zip compression scheme.

J2EE takes the concept of a JAR several steps further. J2EE components are packaged into basic JAR files with one or more deployment descriptor files. Deployment descriptors provide configuration information for the J2EE container.

One or more J2EE components may be packaged into an Enterprise Archive, or EAR file. EARs contain JARs, WARs, and additional descriptor files.

Whether you are building a JAR, WAR, or EAR, all archives follow a similar directory structure and use the same tool for compression.

BASIC JAR CONTENTS

A basic JAR file format consists of the following:

1. A root directory (e.g., C:\basicjar).
2. Subdirectories conforming to the package structure. For example, if the file contained the com.codenotes.j2ee.util package, you would add a directory called C:\ejb\com\codenotes\j2ee\util\. This directory would house the class files for the package.
3. A manifest file (manifest.mf) that is generated by the archive tool.

EJB JAR FILE FORMAT

The file and folder structure for an EJB JAR extends the basic JAR contents by adding:

1. A META-INF directory for configuration files (e.g., C:\ejb\META-INF). This directory name should be capitalized.
2. An "ejb-jar.xml" descriptor file in the META-INF directory. Descriptor files are described in the next topic.
3. Possibly additional vendor-specific deployment descriptors in the META-INF directory.

APPLICATION-CLIENT JAR FORMAT

An application-client follows the Basic JAR format with the following additions:

1. A META-INF directory for configuration files (e.g., C:\app\META-INF).
2. An "application-client.xml" descriptor file.

WAR FILE FORMAT

Web archives are organized along the same lines as regular JAR files but have several added features:

1. The root directory (e.g., C:\webdev)—The WAR root directory houses top-level JSPs, HTML, and other web pages.
2. Subdirectories—Additional directories can be added to conform to the web server page layout. The subdirectories can also contain JSPs, HTML, and other web files.
3. A WEB-INF directory—The WEB-INF directory is hidden from the web server.
4. A web.xml deployment descriptor—This file contains a registry of Servlets and other deployment information.
5. Possibly additional vendor-specific deployment descriptors—Some vendors require additional descriptors for WAR files.
6. A "classes" sub-directory (e.g., C:\webdev\WEB-INF\classes)—This directory holds Servlets, JavaBeans, and other compiled Java classes.
7. A "lib" subdirectory (e.g., C:\webdev\WEB-INF\lib)—This directory holds any required JAR files, such as packaged libraries and database drivers. The Jars in this directory and the "classes" directory are automatically included in the web application's CLASSPATH.

The Web Archive format should look very familiar from the Web Application section of Chapter 2 (Installation).

EAR FILE FORMAT

Enterprise Archives have a simple structure that is very close to that of a basic JAR file:

1. A root directory—The root directory contains J2EE components such as EJB-JAR files, WAR files and application-client JAR files.
2. A META-INF directory—This directory holds the application.xml deployment descriptor.

3. An "application.xml" descriptor—The application descriptor lists the various components of the archive.
4. Possibly additional vendor-specific deployment descriptors.

BUILDING AN ARCHIVE FILE

Once you have built the required file structure and added your components and descriptors, you should compress the archive into a single file. The compression tool works the same way for every type of archive:

```
jar cf archivename[.JAR, .WAR, .EAR] rootDirectory
```

Listing 8.7 The JAR command

For example, if we wanted to build a Web Archive from the directory created in Chapter 2 (Installation), the command would be:

```
jar cf CodeNotes.war c:\webdev
```

The JAR command will recursively add the contents of the C:\webdev directory into the file and create a manifest.

The JAR command can be found in the \bin directory of your Java Developers Kit installation (e.g., C:\jdk1.3\bin).

Topic: Deployment Descriptors

All of the J2EE archive formats use deployment descriptors (DDs) to provide deployment-specific settings. The following descriptions of the deployment descriptors are sometimes hard to follow. As you are reading, feel free to jump to the Example section at the end of each section. The examples provide several common cases and illustrate the XML nature of the DDs.

It's All XML

DDs are written in XML against specific Document Type Definitions (or DTDs), which define the grammar for the document. If you are unfamiliar with XML and DTDs, a quick refresher can be found on the CodeNotes website CN J2080001.

Most of the confusion concerning the configuration of components can be traced to a lack of familiarity with XML. That having been said, there are a few common errors that can cause endless headaches:

- The element order is critically important. The J2EE XML Document Type Definitions require that certain tags be placed in a specific order. Either have a copy of the specific DTD handy or use an XML editor that enforces the DTD structure. This chapter violates this rule in numerous places in order to group logical elements.
- Watch out for syntax errors. Stray spaces, missing brackets, and alternative capitalization can make deployment a nightmare. Similarly, white space and line breaks can also cause problems. Once again, this chapter violates these rules in several places because of size constraints.
- The DTDs for each of these deployment descriptors can be found either online or in the $J2EE_HOME/lib/dtds directory (e.g., C:\j2sdkee1.2.1\lib\dtds). You can open these files with a text editor, XML editor, or most web browsers.

In the following sections, you will see the details of the different descriptor types. Remember that all XML blocks require start and end tags even if the tags do not appear in the descriptions in this book.

ENVIRONMENT SETTINGS

EJB JAR, application-client JAR, and WAR descriptors may all contain environment tags. These tags configure resources and environment settings. The resources and settings can be accessed from within an EJB, application-client, Servlet, or JSP by using JNDI to connect to the J2EE server's naming context.

Although the tags are the same, the environment tag locations are different in each descriptor. Be careful to put each tag in the correct place. There are three types of resource tags:

- <resource-ref>—For resource manager factories, such as a DataSource
    - <res-ref-name>—Arbitrary name of the resource. These names are commonly prefixed with the following paths:
        - JDBC DataSource objects: java:comp/env/jdbc
        - JMS ConnectionFactory objects: java:comp/env/jms

        ▪JavaMail sessions: java:comp/env/mail
    - <res-type>—Fully qualified class name of the factory (e.g., `javax.sql.Datasource`)
    - <res-auth>—Either "application" or "container"; identifies who will sign in to the resource
- <ejb-ref>—If an application-client, EJB, or Web Archive references an EJB, the EJB must be listed in the environment.
    - <ejb-ref-name>—Arbitrary name for this reference, generally "ejb/" followed by EJB name
    - <ejb-ref-type>—"entity" or "session"
    - <home>—Fully qualified class name for home interface
    - <remote>—Fully qualified class name for remote interface
    - <ejb-link>—Name of EJB defined in the same JAR or in a JAR inside the same application
- <env-entry> (0 or more)—These tags store default primitive values.
    - <env-entry-name>—Name of variable
    - <env-entry-type>—Must be primitive wrapper class (`java.lang.Integer`, `java.lang.Float`, `java.lang.String`, etc.)
    - <env-entry-value>—Default value

Example

A typical set of environment tags might include:

```
<!-- A JDBC Datasource -->
<resource-ref>
  <res-ref-name>jdbc/MyDatasourc</res-ref-name>
  <res-type>javax.sql.DataSource</res-type>
  <res-auth>application</res-auth>
</resource-ref>
<!-- An EJB resource -->
<ejb-ref>
  <ejb-ref-name>ejb/AccountHomeRef</ejb-ref-name>
  <ejb-ref-type>Entity</ejb-ref-type>
  <home>com.codenotes.j2ee.ejb.AccountHome</home>
  <remote>com.codenotes.j2ee.ejb.AccountRemote</remote>
  <ejb-link>Account</ejb-link>
<ejb-ref>
<!-- A String value -->
<env-entry>
  <env-entry-name>ClientName</env-entry-name>
```

```
  <env-entry-type>java.lang.String</env-entry-type>
  <env-entry-value>CodeNotes</env-entry-value>
</env-entry>
```

Listing 8.8 Environment tags

EJB DEPLOYMENT DESCRIPTORS

Each EJB JAR file must contain a deployment descriptor named "ejb-jar.xml". The header for an ejb-jar.xml file is:

```
<?xml version="1.0" encoding="ISO-8859-1"?>
<!-- remove line breaks from !DOCTYPE tag -->
<!DOCTYPE ejb-jar PUBLIC
  "-//Sun Microsystems, Inc.//DTD Enterprise JavaBeans 1.1//EN"
  "http://java.sun.com/j2ee/dtds/ejb-jar_1_1.dtd" >
```

Listing 8.9 EJB header

Each ejb-jar.xml file is encapsulated in an <ejb-jar> tag. EJB deployment descriptors have several sections:

- Header tags—These tags (<description>,<display-name>, <small-icon>, <large-icon>) are all optional and provide display information about the EJB JAR.
- <enterprise-beans>—The first required section describes the beans and their environment.
- <assembly-descriptor>—This section defines container-managed transactions, security roles, method permissions, and security role references.
- <ejb-client-jar> (optional)—This tag contains the name of the separate JAR file with the classes required by a client application.

The <enterprise-beans> and <assembly-descriptor> tags are the most important sections of this descriptor.

<enterprise-beans>

The <enterprise-beans> tag contains a description of every bean in the JAR file. This container tag contains an <entity> or <session> entry for every bean inside the EJB JAR. Entity beans are listed with <entity> tags and session beans are listed with <session> tags.

Both <entity> and <session> tags share some common elements:

- <ejb-name>—An arbitrary name (alias) to refer to this EJB. A physical EJB can be deployed more than once inside a JAR with different security, environment, and/or transaction settings, provided that the ejb-name is unique for each instance of the bean.
- <home>—Fully qualified class name of the home interface
- <remote>—Fully qualified class name of the remote interface
- <ejb-class>—Fully qualified class name of the bean implementation
- <security-role-ref>—If a bean uses programmatic security, you must declare the roles, and possibly link them to declarative roles. See the Security topic for more details.

In addition, <session> entries have two additional required tags:

- <session-type>—"Stateful" or "stateless"
- <transaction-type>—"Bean" or "container." The "bean" setting implies that the bean will handle all transaction initiations internally. Otherwise, the container will use the declarative transaction attributes defined in the <assembly-descriptor> below.

Entity beans have several additional required tags:

- <persistence-type>—"Bean" or "container"
- <prim-key-class>—Fully qualified class name for the primary key class
- <reentrant>—This tag indicates whether loopback calls are allowed (i.e., can A call B, which calls A?). It can be True or False.

If you are using Container-Managed Persistence with an entity bean, you will also need a <cmp-field><field-name> tag structure for every public field that will be stored in the database, including the primary key. For example, a user bean with public name, phone, and e-mail fields would have tags like:

```
<cmp-field><field-name>name</field-name></cmp-field>
<cmp-field><field-name>phone</field-name></cmp-field>
<cmp-field><field-name>email</field-name></cmp-field>
```

Listing 8.10 CMP field descriptor

<assembly-descriptor>

The <assembly-descriptor> tag configures the transaction and security settings for all EJBs defined in the <enterprise-beans> tag. The assembly descriptor has three main tags.

- <security-role><role-name> (0 or more)—Identifies a security role for the JAR file. See Security topic for more details.
- <container-transaction> (0 or more)—Applies a transaction attribute to one or more methods
    - <method> (1 or more)—Identifies method(s)
    - <trans-attribute>—Transaction attribute applied to all of the methods. Must be one of: `NotSupported`, `Supports`, `Required`, `RequiresNew`, `Mandatory`, `Never`. See Transactions topic in Chapter 7.
- <method-permission> (0 or more)—Links methods and roles together in order to define permissions for method execution
    - <role-name> (1 or more)—Name of a defined security role
    - <method> (1 or more)—Method identifier

Both <method-permission> and <container-transaction> use the same <method> identifier tag. This tag has two required subtags and several optional ones:

- <ejb-name> (required)—Name of an EJB identified in the <enterprise-beans> section
- <method-name> (required)—Name of the method as defined in the EJB interface. This can be set to "*", which indicates all of the public methods for the EJB.
- <method-params> (optional)—If you need to differentiate between overloaded methods, you can add a parameter list.[1]
    - <method-param> (1 or more)—Name of the parameter

Example

```
<?xml version="1.0"?>
<!--remove linebreaks from !DOCTYPE -->
<!DOCTYPE ejb-jar PUBLIC
  "-//Sun Microsystems, Inc.//DTD Enterprise JavaBeans 1.1//EN"
  "http://java.sun.com/j2ee/dtds/ejb-jar_1_1.dtd">
<ejb-jar>
  <enterprise-beans>
```

1. The list may contain one or more <method-param> tags, identifying the arguments in the overlooked method.

```
    <session>
      <ejb-name>Calculator</ejb-name>
      <home>CalculatorHome</home>
      <remote>Calculator</remote>
      <ejb-class>CalculatorBean</ejb-class>
      <session-type>Stateless</session-type>
      <transaction-type>Container</transaction-type>
    </session>
  </enterprise-beans>
</ejb-jar>
```

Listing 8.11 A typical EJB deployment descriptor

APPLICATION–CLIENT DEPLOYMENT

Application-client JARs must contain a descriptor called "application-client.xml". This descriptor is actually very simple and includes many of the sections described in the EJB descriptor. The header for a application-client.xml file is:

```
<?XML version="1.0" encoding="ISO-8859-1"?>
<!--remove linebreaks from !DOCTYPE -->
<!DOCTYPE application-client PUBLIC
  "-//Sun Microsystems, Inc.//DTD Application Client 1.2//EN"
  "http://java.sun.com/j2ee/dtds/application-client_1.2.dtd" >
```

Listing 8.12 Application-client header

Each application-client descriptor must be encapsulated in <application-client> tags and contain the following sections:

1. <icon> (optional)—This tag points to a GIF or JPG that will be used to identify the client.
2. <display-name>—A short name that is displayed by deployment tools.
3. <description> (optional)—A section for comments.

The application client also has the same environment tags described for EJB descriptors in the Environment Settings section (<env-entry>, <env-ref>, <resource-ref>.

Example

```
<?XML version="1.0" encoding="ISO-8859-1"?>
<!--remove linebreaks from !DOCTYPE -->
<!DOCTYPE application-client PUBLIC
  "-//Sun Microsystems, Inc.//DTD Application Client 1.2//EN"
  "http://java.sun.com/j2ee/dtds/application-client_1.2.dtd" >
<application-client>
  <display-name>MyClient</display-name>
  <description>A simple client</description>
  <!-- Env tags removed for brevity -->
```

Listing 8.13 A typical application-client deployment descriptor

WEB ARCHIVE DEPLOYMENT

Each WAR file must have a "web.xml" deployment descriptor. You have already seen this descriptor in action when you registered Servlets in Chapter 5. The header for a web.xml file is:

```
<?XML version="1.0" encoding="ISO-8859-1"?>
<!--remove linebreaks from !DOCTYPE -->
<!DOCTYPE web-app PUBLIC
  "-//Sun Microsystems, Inc.//DTD Web Application 2.2//EN"
  "http://java.sun.com/j2ee/dtds/web-app_2.2.dtd" >
```

Listing 8.14 Web Archive header

Each web descriptor must be encapsulated in <web-app> tags. Most of the web.xml tags are self-evident from the DTD. Like the application-client archive and the EJB archive, the Web Archive also has environment tags (<env-entry>, <ejb-ref>, <resource-ref>). The interesting tags fall into three categories:

1. Container configuration
2. Servlet and JSP configuration
3. Environment and security

These groups are explained in the following sections.

Container Configuration

Many of the container configuration parameters are accessible through the Servlet support objects and JSP implicit objects.

- <distributable> (optional)—If this tag is present, then the WAR is programmed to be deployed into a distributed Servlet container. This means that all the rules for sharing across multiple virtual machines have been followed CN J2080002.
- <context-param> (0 or more)—Used for setting application scope parameters that can be accessed by Servlets or JSP pages
    - <param-name>—Name of parameter
    - <param-value>—Value of parameter
- <session-config><session-timeout> (optional)—Sets default session timeout in minutes
- <mime-mapping> (0 or more)—Builds a mapping between a MIME file type and an extension
    - <extension>—File extension (e.g., "txt")
    - <mime-type>—MIME type (e.g., "text/plain")
- <welcome-file-list> (optional)—List of default files[2]
- <error-page> (0 or more)—List of special pages for different HTML error codes or Java exceptions
    - <error-code | exception-type>—Error code number (e.g., 404) or exception type (java.sql.SQLException)
    - <location>—Name of page that will handle the error

Servlet and JSP Registration

Servlets must be registered in the web.xml file, and JSPs may be registered. Servlet registration was first discussed in Chapter 5.

- <Servlet> (0 or more)—Used for naming Servlet classes or JSPs
    - <Servlet-name>—Arbitrary name of the Servlet or JSP page
    - <Servlet-class | jsp-file>—Contains the fully qualified class name of the Servlet, or complete path to the JSP file
    - <init-param> (0 or more)—You can pass initialization parameters to a Servlet or JSP's `init()` function using these tags. The parameters will be available as part of the `javax.Servlet.ServletConfig` parameter.
        - <param-name>—Name of the parameter
        - <param-value>—Parameter value
    - <load-on-startup> (optional)—This tag will force a Servlet to be loaded when the application is started, rather than on first use. The tag may contain an integer number. Lower integers will load first. If no number is present, the container will determine the startup order.
- <Servlet-mapping> (0 or more)—Maps Servlets or JSPs to a

2. Containing one or more <welcome-file> tags indicating the startup web page (e.g., index.html)

particular URL. You can use this to hide your Servlet names or to mask the fact that you are using JSP.

  - <Servlet-name>—Name of a Servlet or JSP identified in a <Servlet> tag
  - <url-pattern>—Relative URL name for the Servlet or JSP page

- <taglib> (0 or more)—Used to identify JSP tag libraries. Tag libraries are covered on the CodeNotes website CN J2060001.
  - <taglib-uri>—Location of the taglib, relative to the root directory
  - <taglib-location>—Path to the taglib file

Environment and Security

The environment tags are the same as those used for EJBs. The <security-constraint> tags define a set of pages, a set of allowed roles, and a transport mechanism for access.

- <web-resource-collection>
  - <web-resource-name>—Arbitrary name for the collection
  - <url-pattern> (0 or more)—URL to a page in the web application
  - <http-method> (0 or more)—HTTP method, which is generally GET, POST, or PUT. If tag is missing, all methods are allowed

Note that a web-resource-collection can contain any number of pages. The HTTP-method restriction applies to every page in the collection.

- <auth-constraint>—This tag provides basic access to the web-resource-collection for one or more roles.[3]

Note that more than one role can be assigned to any collection.

- <user-data-constraint>—Used to identify transport guarantees[4]

The user-data-constraint method defines a limit on how data is transferred between the client and the server:

3. The authorized role names are included in one or more <role-name> tags. The roles must be defined in a separate <security-role> tag.

4. Each guarantee is contained in a <transport-guarantee> tag and must be NONE, INTEGRAL, or CONFIDENTIAL.

- NONE—No limits are placed on the transfer.
- INTEGRAL—The data must be transferred in an unalterable method.
- CONFIDENTIAL—The data must be transferred in a way that it cannot be accessed except by the client and server.

Generally, INTEGRAL and CONFIDENTIAL imply the use of HTTPS, SSL, or some other secure transfer method.

Example

```
<?xml version="1.0" encoding="ISO-8859-1"?>
<!--remove linebreaks from !DOCTYPE -->
<!DOCTYPE web-app PUBLIC
  "-//Sun Microsystems, Inc.//DTD Web Application 2.2//EN"
  "http://java.sun.com/j2ee/dtds/web-app_2.2.dtd">
<web-app>
  <servlet>
    <servlet-name>
      HelloServlet
    </servlet-name>
    <servlet-class>
      HelloServlet
    </servlet-class>
  </servlet>
  <servlet-mapping>
    <servlet-name>
      HelloServlet
    </servlet-name>
    <url-pattern>
      /HelloServlet
    </url-pattern>
  </servlet-mapping>
</web-app>
```

Listing 8.15 A typical web application deployment descriptor

ENTERPRISE APPLICATION DEPLOYMENT

Enterprise Archives must contain an "application.xml" file, which is the smallest of the descriptors. The header for an application.xml file is:

```
<?XML version="1.0" encoding="ISO-8859-1"?>
<!--remove linebreaks from !DOCTYPE -->
<!DOCTYPE application PUBLIC
  "-//Sun Microsystems, Inc.//DTD J2EE Application 1.2//EN"
  "http://java.sun.com/j2ee/dtds/application_1_2.dtd">
```

Listing 8.16 Enterprise Archive header

Application descriptors are encapsulated in <application> tags and contain the usual header sections (<icon>, <display-name>, <description>), <modules>, and <security-role>. Security roles are discussed in the Security topic later in this chapter.

<modules>

A module is a component consisting of an EJB JAR, an application-client JAR, or a Web Archive. The <module> tag contains one of three subtags, and possibly an <alt-dd> tag containing the path to the deployment descriptor for the component.

- <ejb>—Name of EJB JAR file
- <java>—Name of application-client JAR
- <web>—used for WAR files
  - <web-uri>—Name of WAR file
  - <context-root>—Name of context-root for application (in Chapters 5 and 6, the context root was "CodeNotes")

Example

```
<?xml version="1.0"?>
<!--remove linebreaks from !DOCTYPE -->
<!DOCTYPE application PUBLIC
  '-//Sun Microsystems, Inc.//DTD J2EE Application 1.2//EN'
  'http://java.sun.com/j2ee/dtds/application_1_2.dtd'>
<application>
  <display-name>CalculatorApplication</display-name>
  <description>A simple calculator.</description>
  <module>
    <ejb>Calculator.jar</ejb>
  </module>
</application>
```

Listing 8.17 A typical enterprise application deployment descriptor

Chapter Summary

At this point, you may feel overwhelmed by deployment descriptors, archive files, and XML tags. However, the entire deployment chapter can be summarized in a few key points:

1. Most J2EE servers provide some tools to help you build the XML. You will rarely need to build all of the deployment descriptors by hand.
2. Except in rare circumstances, you do not need to worry about security during code development. The exceptions are programmatic role-checking in EJBs, JSPs and Servlets.
3. Role-based security is your friend. It is easy to build and very easy to maintain. If a business rule changes, requiring a different security policy, simply adjust the deployment descriptors.

Chapter 9

DARKSIDE

WHAT'S IN A VERSION NUMBER?

One of the most common complaints about Java in general and J2EE in particular is that no one is sure which version number they should be employing. Not only does Java itself have a number (currently 2), but every component in Java, including the development environments, has an independent version and revision number.

The easiest way to find out exactly which component version is part of a particular environment (e.g., J2EE 1.2.1) is to read the specification, which can be downloaded from Sun (e.g., java.sun.com/j2ee/download .html#platformspec).

EJB DEPLOYMENT AND CONFIGURATION TOOLS

Enterprise JavaBeans, while powerful, require a certain amount of drudge work in building the interfaces and callback methods. A lot of this monotony can be helped by using a code generation tool such as EJBGen, available at www.beust.com/cedric/ejbgen/. EJBGen is a doclet library, using the javadoc format of providing keywords inside Java comments to provide "hints" about various properties of the EJB. It generates EJB standard deployment descriptors and descriptors for BEA WebLogic 6.x.

Another approach is to edit the XML deployment descriptors with an XML editor. Such an editor will take an XML schema or DTD and provide the outline structure of the XML document that you are writing. It provides a "fill in the blanks" approach that simplifies the process of configuring web applications and EJBs. Several XML editors exist, which can be found through industry resource sites like `www.xml.com/`.

Our preferred tool is TurboXML from TIBCO Extensibility (`www.extensibility.com/`).

Building and Deployment

The Apache Jakarta project's Ant tool (jakarta.apache.org/ant/index.html) is a software building tool similar to the UNIX "make" command. The primary difference is that it uses an XML configuration file. It is easily extensible to perform automatic deployments to various J2EE servers.

TESTING AND PERFORMANCE OPTIMIZATION

Testing business logic developed in regular Java code or Enterprise JavaBeans requires (at the very least) a tool for performing "white box" assertion tests on all features of your system. We recommend the open source tool JUnit. The JUnit homepage, (www.junit.org/) also has plenty of articles on testing J2EE components and links to various J2EE JUnit extensions that make testing a less painful experience.

Many performance bottlenecks are not immediately easy to find. Java profiling or monitoring tools can often help track the problems. The following are the top tools that integrate with most J2EE application servers:

- Sitraka JProbe ServerSide Suite—www.sitraka.com/software/jprobe/jprobeserverside.html
- OptimizeIt—www.optimizeit.com/

Setting Up the Debugger

The Java Platform Debugger Architecture (JPDA) is built into the JRE 1.3 and can operate inside most Java-based J2EE servers. The debugger provides an interface inside the server for tracing through objects (EJBs, Servlets, JSPs), setting break points, and accessing stack traces.

The command for starting the JDPA is:

```
java -Xnoagent -Xdebug -Djava.compiler=NONE
  -Xrunjdwp:transport=(dt_socket|dt_shmem),
```

```
address=([host:]port|"shmem symbol"), server=y, suspend=(y|n),
  ClassName
```

Listing 9.1 Starting the debugger

More information about the JPDA, including vendor-specific examples, can be found on the CodeNotes site CN J209001.

J2EE 1.3 SPECIFICATION

For more complete commentary on the J2EE 1.3 specification, check the CodeNotes website CN J2090002.

JDBC 3.0

Although JDBC 3.0 is part of the next release of the J2SE (JDK 1.4), the next J2EE release will only require JDBC 2.2. However, neither of these releases significantly affects the core JDBC functionality. Most of the changes deal with improvements to the `javax.sql.DataSource` interface, connection pooling, and driver specification.

Servlets 2.3

The updated Servlet specification contains a defined method for "Servlet Filtering" or chaining several Servlets in a transparent fashion.

JSP 1.2

The new draft of JSP contains added features for custom tag libraries.

EJB 2.0

Of all of the APIs, the EJB specification will change the most. These are some of the more important changes:

- NEW: Message-driven beans. These beans are a new variety of stateless bean that subscribes to a JMS topic or queue through the deployment descriptor. These beans do not have home or remote interfaces or interceptors, and can only be called through JMS.
- NEW: Home method names. With the new specification, you can deletage regular methods on the home interface to `ejbHomeXXXX`().
- CHANGED: `create()` methods on home interfaces can now use larger method names, i.e., `createXXXX()`.
- NEW: Transaction and Security are now interoperable among heterogeneous EJB servers.

- NEW: `EJBLocalObject` and `EJBLocalHome`. These local EJBs are not RMI objects and should be used mainly for entity beans. Also note that an EJB can expose BOTH a remote and local interface. The interceptor will determine whether arguments are passed by reference (local) or by `Serialization` (remote).
- CHANGED: Container-Managed Persistence entity beans may only use the Required, RequiresNew, and Mandatory transaction types.
- CHANGED: A bean can "<run-as>" a particular security role, configured in the deployment descriptor (this was in EJB 1.0, taken away in 1.1, now back again). That means you can "cloak" or "stealth" your bean actions.
- NEW: Container-Managed Persistence now supports:
    - One-to-one, one-to-many, many-to-one, and many-to-many relationships among entity beans
    - Multiobject relationships, which can be either `java.util.Collection` or `java.util.Set` classes
    - Referential integrity among relationships, which can be preserved if an object is added to one side of the relationship
    - Abstract fields using get/set methods (i.e., no public fields required or used)
    - Cascade-delete on private relationships (one-to-one and one-to-many)
    - EJB QL, an SQL-like object-oriented query language that provides standardized finder-method queries in deployment descriptors
    - ejbSelect calls—Like finders, but for private internal use of the EJB's business methods

Index

The *f* after a number refers to a figure, *t* refers to a table, and *l* refers to a listing of code.